"Where No One Has Gone Before"™

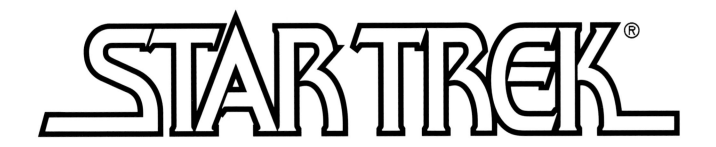

STAR TREK®

"Where No One Has Gone Before"™

A HISTORY IN PICTURES

Text by

J.M. Dillard

Additional Material by

Susan Sackett

Terry J. Erdmann

Judith and Garfield Reeves-Stevens

John Ordover

Photo Consultants

Paula Block

Tyya Turner

POCKET BOOKS

New York   London   Toronto   Sydney   Tokyo   Singapore

Acknowledgments

Like its subject, this book was a group effort. It could not have been completed without the help of the following cheerful, stalwart souls: Susan Sackett, John Ordover, Paula Block, Tyya Turner, Terry Erdmann, and Judith and Garfield Reeves-Stevens.

They have my deepest gratitude.

So do Leonard Nimoy, Jeri Taylor, Dorothy Fontana, and Marc Okrand, who graciously shared their time and unique perspectives on STAR TREK.

Most of all, my thanks go to Kevin Ryan, who served as fearless leader, coordinator, photo gatherer, and infinite font of information. Let out a long, deep sigh, Kev. This one's finally finished.

Thanks to the many people at Paramount Pictures who made special contributions to this book: Rick Berman, Michael Piller, Ronald D. Moore, Brannon Braga, Robert Blackman, Zayra Cabot, Nathan Crowley, Dan Curry, Wendy Drapanas, Doug Drexler, Kim Fitzgerald, Cheryl Gluckstern, Merri Howard, Gary Hutzel, Richard James, Alan Kobayashi, David Livingston, Jim Magdaleno, Jim Mees, Dave Rossi, Guy Vardaman and Herman Zimmerman.

Special thanks to William Shatner, Harve Bennett, Richard Arnold, Michael Okuda, Rick Sternbach, Denise Okuda, Matthew Block, Mike Coates, James Doohan, Jeff Erdmann, Mary Jo Fernandez, Steve Horch, DeForest Kelley, Greg Jein, Mark Lenard, Don Levy, Dan Madsen, Ellen Pasternack, Josh Rose at VisionArt, Alex Singer, James Wang, Ken Whitmore, Gene Trindl, Tom Zimberoff, Jeff Katz, Stephen Poe, Russ Galen, Vicki Birnberg, Jonathan Harris, David Mack, Jean Krevor, Bill Cattell, Chris Adams, Elizabeth Greenberg, Keith DeCandido, and Diane Castro, Jolynn Baca and Stacy Davis at Bender, Goldman & Helper.

And very special thanks to Donna Ruvituso and Richard Oriolo for guidance, patience, and hard work throughout this project.

Contents

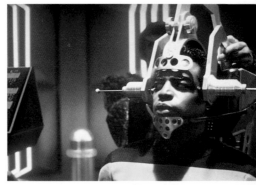

Introduction

I'm in a precarious position because there is no room to sit on Nature's slag heap in the Nevada desert. I'm squatting here to write the introduction for this book and I'm filled with a confusion of emotions.

We are shooting the last scene in which Captain Kirk will ever appear in STAR TREK, and it seems fitting that while I peer at the beautiful pictures of the history of STAR TREK, the sun is burning a hole in my head and the volcanic rock cuts my fingers. Between the extraordinary physical discomfort of the surroundings and the rush of memories that flood through me, a balance between the physical and spiritual has been achieved. The desert wind turns the pages of the book without any help from me just as the STAR TREK story will continue without any help from Captain James T. Kirk. Sorrow engulfs me as I say goodbye to this beloved character.

This book tells some of the story of STAR TREK. Some of the pictures have been seen many times before, others never. All add up to a pictorial chronology of a phenomenon that started in 1966 and is going full blast in 1994 with *Star Trek: The Next Generation, Star Trek: Deep Space Nine* and now *Star Trek: Voyager.*

Looking at these photographs takes me back to the youth that was—to the camaraderie that I shared with the other cast members, the joy of the acting challenges, of playing two characters at the same time, aging beyond recognition, being a Nazi Kirk, fighting a lizard, making love to some of the most beautiful women in Hollywood. This was tough stuff. . . . How about playing a woman in a man's body for a sense-memory exercise?

From these to the jokes we played on one another and the deaths and births that happened as time sped on. It is a fact that I deliberately don't keep photos of events that occur in my life, mostly because, I think, I don't want to see the harsh reality of the passage of time etched in the unforgiving stills.

But here, forced by other hands to see the changes of some thirty years, I peer back into my history with the mixture of a lifetime of feelings. I enjoyed looking at this book for a multitude of reasons. I hope you will find your own reasons to look through this book and enjoy it too.

William Shatner
Valley of Fire, Nevada
June 3, 1994

Tom Zimberoff

For

GENE RODDENBERRY

and all those who, along with him,
have brought the magic of
STAR TREK
to life

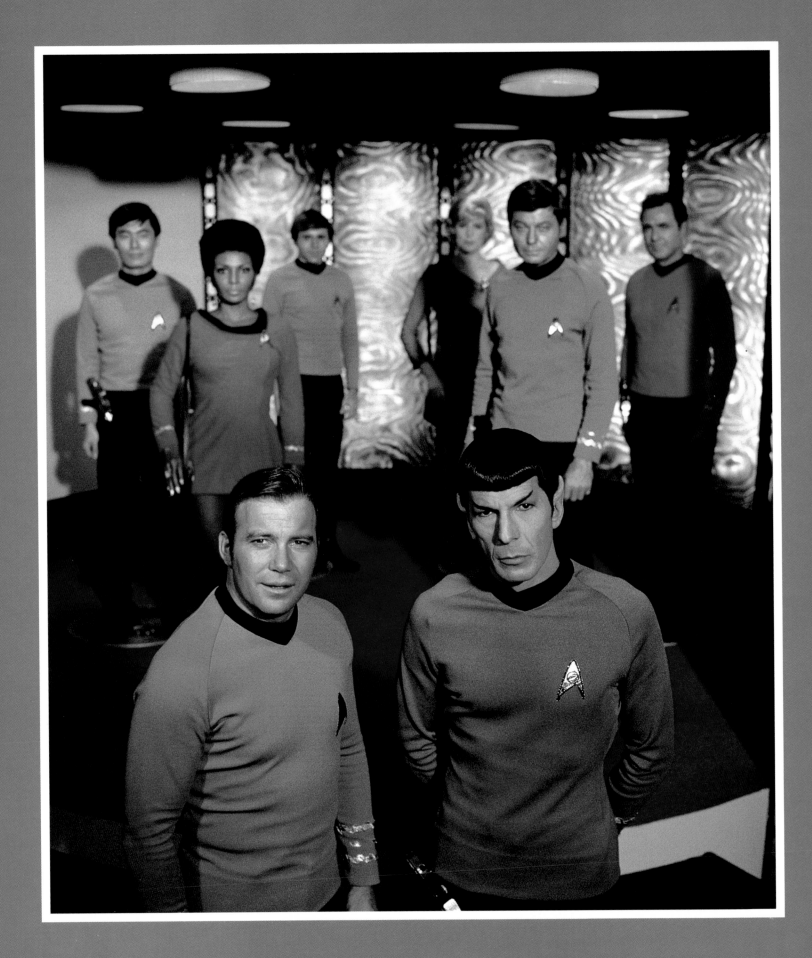

Part One

STAR TREK®

THE ORIGINAL SERIES

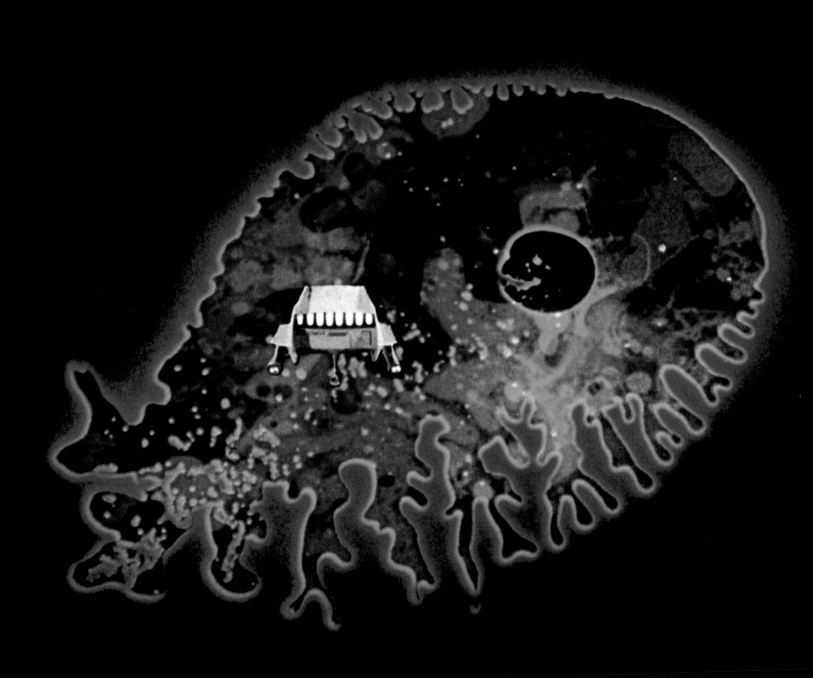

**What I principally take credit for is, I surrounded
myself with a group of very talented, creative
individuals, from the art director, to the costume,
wardrobe designer, the actors who took my
"skeletons" of Spock and Kirk and really put flesh on
the skeleton and made 'em work . . . Television sort
of is the exception to the rule that a committee never
created anything. The committee in this case does
need leadership, but it is a group effort.**

—Gene Roddenberry

The story of STAR TREK rightly begins August 19, 1921, in El Paso, Texas, where Eugene Wesley Roddenberry was born. A sickly but imaginative child, Roddenberry read voraciously—Edgar Rice Burroughs's Mars novels, science fiction in *Astounding Stories* magazine. As he grew older, both his health and his imagination continued to improve. Bitten early by the writing bug, he served as a B-17 bomber pilot during World War II, using his off-duty moments to pen aviation magazine articles and poetry, some of which he sold to *The New York Times.*

After the war, Roddenberry became an international airline pilot for Pan American World Airways, but the urge to write never left him. He continued to produce magazine articles and dreamt of going to Hollywood to launch a career as a writer.

In 1949, he gave in to his dream: he quit his pilot's job and moved to Los Angeles, hoping to write for the new medium of television. In the meantime, he paid the rent by joining the Los Angeles Police Department. Even there his talent for stringing words together didn't go unnoticed, and he began writing speeches for then Chief of Police William Parker.

Eventually, Roddenberry procured an agent and began selling scripts to TV series. Soon after, when he realized that he was earning far more as a script writer than as a cop, he turned in his badge and began writing full-time. A number of script sales followed—to "Dragnet," "Playhouse 90," "Naked City," and "Doctor Kildare," among others. In due time, he landed a job as story editor on "Have Gun, Will Travel"; his script for that series' episode "Helen of Abajnian" won him the prestigious Writers' Guild Award.

In 1959, he turned to producing, for as he said, "it became apparent to me that if you want the film to reflect accurately what you felt when you wrote the script, then you have to produce it, too." His first few pilots failed to sell (one of them, "333 Montgomery," starred DeForest Kelley). Finally, he sold the Marine Corps drama "The Lieutenant," which featured Gary Lockwood and Robert Vaughn. (Actors Leonard Nimoy, Nichelle Nichols, Walter Koenig, Grace Lee Whitney, and Majel Barrett all guest-starred on the series.)

The man at the helm: Gene Roddenberry on the original U.S.S. Enterprise bridge set

"The Lieutenant" only lasted one season, and as it was gearing down, Roddenberry's thoughts turned to his next series—and the future. At that time, he was greatly influenced by a recent nonfiction book, Arthur C. Clarke's *Profiles of the Future,* which discussed "space drive," "warped space," and "instantaneous transportation." Inspired, Roddenberry decided that his next series would be a science-fiction show. "Now," he said, "perhaps I'd be able to talk about love, war, nature, God, sex . . . and maybe the TV censors would let it pass because it all seemed so make-believe."

Thus STAR TREK was born. Roddenberry's original concept was that of a "Wagon Train to the Stars," and included the *Starship Yorktown* plus significantly different characters from the ones we know today: ship's captain Robert April, the logical female second-in-command Number One, navigator Jose Tyler, captain's yeoman J. M. Colt, and elderly Dr. Philip Boyce. And as for Mr. Spock . . .

According to Samuel A. Peeples, writer of the episode "Where No Man Has Gone Before," "Spock was [originally] a red-skinned creature with fiery ears, who had a plate in the middle of his stomach. He didn't eat or drink, but he fed upon any form of energy that struck this plate in his stomach. I told Gene that I thought this very effectively destroyed him as an interesting character because he was no longer human and that he should be at least half-human and have the problems of both sides."

Unfortunately, MGM, who had backed "The Lieutenant," didn't think science fiction would appeal to 1960s viewers. Roddenberry shopped his series concept to several studios, but all rejected it as too risky and expensive—all except Desilu, which was actively seeking new projects and signed Roddenberry to a three-year deal.

With Desilu's backing, Roddenberry started pitching his new show to the networks. He began with CBS executives, who, after pumping him for information about his new science-fiction idea, informed him they already

had a more "adult" science-fiction series in the works, named "Lost in Space." But NBC was interested, and commissioned a pilot.

Roddenberry developed three story ideas; of them, NBC chose "The Cage," and so Roddenberry set to work on the pilot script. In September 1964, the network approved the script, and the first STAR TREK pilot was under way.

The captain's name had been changed from Robert April to Christopher Pike (and the ship's name from the *Yorktown* to the *Enterprise*), but otherwise the cast of characters adhered to the original format. Roddenberry approached Lloyd Bridges of "Sea Hunt" fame to play the lead, but when Bridges turned him down, Jeffrey Hunter was chosen to play Captain Pike. Veteran character actor John Hoyt was cast as Dr. Phillip Boyce, and Majel Barrett as the frosty, logical Number One.

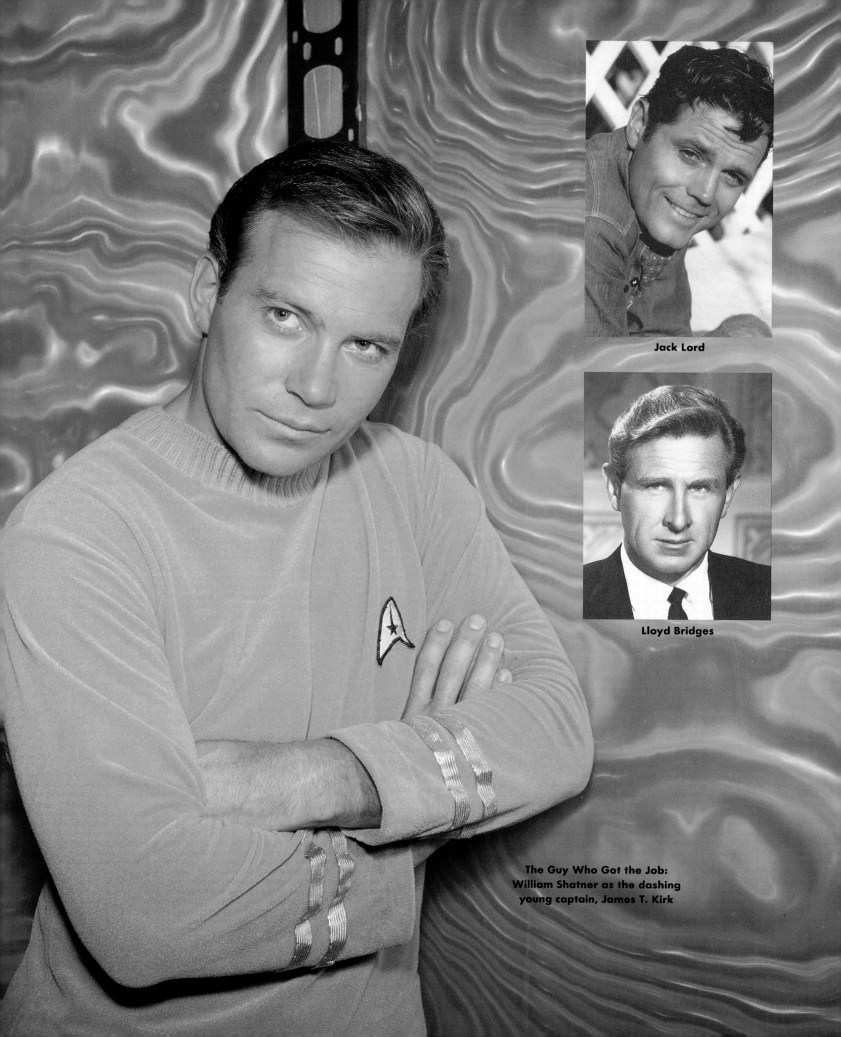

Jack Lord

Lloyd Bridges

The Guy Who Got the Job:
William Shatner as the dashing
young captain, James T. Kirk

Casting the Captain

From the beginning, Roddenberry knew exactly what sort of man should captain the *Starship Enterprise*. "Like any writer," he said, "all the characters came out of pieces of me. [The captain] was the sort of eternally cool, resourceful airline pilot I wish I'd been." According to the original STAR TREK bible, Captain Robert M. April, was "about thirty-four, Academy graduate, rank of captain. Clearly the leading man and central character. This role is designated for an actor of top repute and ability. A shorthand sketch of Robert April might be 'a space-age Captain Horatio Hornblower,' lean and capable both mentally and physically. . . .

"A colorfully complex personality, he is capable of action and decision which can verge on the heroic—and at the same time lives a continual battle with self-doubt and the loneliness of command.

"As with similar men in the past (Drake, Cook, Bougainville and Scott), his primary weakness is a predilection to action over administration, a temptation to take the greatest risks onto himself."

Roddenberry clearly knew his character well. But finding the right actor to fill the role—well, that was another matter altogether, particularly since Gene's first choice was unavailable.

"I remember being turned down by Lloyd Bridges of 'Sea Hunt,'" he recalled. "It wasn't a foolish move on his part. I was talking what sounded like a lot of nonsense in those days. He had said, 'I've seen science fiction, Gene, and it doesn't work.' Judging by most of the science fiction around, I had to agree with him.

"We went through a lot of film in casting the part. Jeff Hunter seemed to be about the closest to what I had in mind for a captain."

Best known for his portrayal of Jesus in the film *King of Kings,* Hunter was the last of the principals cast. But when NBC rejected the first pilot, Hunter chose not to return to STAR TREK as Christopher Pike, and Roddenberry was once again looking for a captain. The next person called was Jack Lord, who went on to star in "Hawaii Five-0." But Lord insisted on fifty-percent ownership of the show, and that was unacceptable to both Roddenberry and Desilu Studios. So the search continued and then settled on a young actor named William Shatner.

Shatner was well respected for his work on episodes of "The Twilight Zone" and "The Outer Limits," as well as on an unsold television pilot, "Alexander the Great." When Roddenberry called,

Shatner had just finished a television series, "For the People," and was unemployed. The timing couldn't have been better. Together, Shatner and Roddenberry viewed the first STAR TREK pilot. "I thought it was wonderful," Shatner says. "I saw some of the magic that I thought was a possibility. . . ."

But he also felt that the characters were taking themselves far too seriously. He suggested that it would be better to lighten the captain up. Roddenberry agreed, and so the tormented "self-doubt" mentioned in the original Robert April bio was dispensed with.

Shatner based the character Kirk on Horatio Hornblower, and also on Alexander the Great, the hero from his previous pilot. He says, "Alexander was the epitome of the Greek hero. He was the athlete and the intellectual of his time . . . a great warrior and a great thinker. . . . I saw something of Kirk in Alexander—the heroism . . . [the striking out] into unknown territories."

He also admits that there's more than a little bit of Bill Shatner in James T. Kirk, "if only because in seventy-nine shows, day after day, week after week, year after year, the fatigue factor is such that you can only try to be as honest about yourself as possible. Fatigue wipes away any subterfuge that you might be able to use as an actor in character roles, or trying to delineate something that might not be entirely you. By the second week you're so tired that it can only be you, so I think that in Kirk there's a great deal of me."

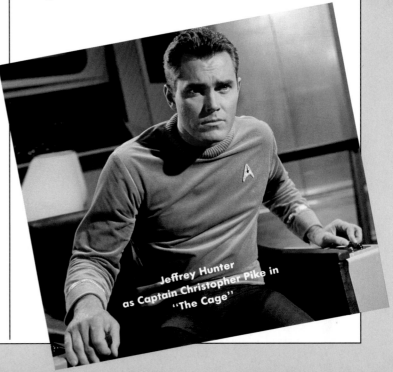

Jeffrey Hunter as Captain Christopher Pike in "The Cage"

Crewman Tyler, Mr. Spock, and Dr. Boyce search for their missing captain on the surface of Talos IV

Captain Pike suffers in "hell," courtesy of the Talosians' power of illusion

Leonard Nimoy, of course, had always been Roddenberry's first choice for the part of Spock; he had wanted to cast the actor as an alien ever since he saw Nimoy perform in "The Lieutenant." Had Nimoy refused the role, Roddenberry said, "I probably would've gotten Marty [Martin] Landau. I'd worked with him. I had him in mind as a possibility."

When Nimoy was called to meet with Roddenberry, the actor assumed he would have to compete against others for a role in the new show, and was surprised to learn otherwise. Says Nimoy, "Gene showed me around the studio. He showed me the sets that were being developed and the wardrobe that was being designed . . . I began to realize that he was selling me on the idea of being in this series—unusual for an actor. I figured all I had to do was keep my mouth shut and I might end up with a good job here."

One thing Roddenberry wanted in his pilot was a green dancing woman, so Majel Barrett was used to screen-test the green makeup that would later be worn by the female guest star. She recalls, "The makeup they put on me was as green as green can be, but they kept sending out the rushes and we would get it back the next day, and there I was just as pink and rosy as could possibly be. So they decided there was not enough green in it—I got greener and greener. Now, this stuff is hard to get off. I rubbed my face raw. This went on for three days, until they finally called the lab and said, 'What do we have to do to get this woman's face green?' And they said, 'Green? You *wanted* it green? We thought it was a mistake, so we've been color-correcting!'"

Susan Oliver was finally cast as Vina, the female guest star, and the pilot was shot in nine days at a cost of $630,000, which at that time made it the most expensive pilot ever produced. Despite the cost, NBC rejected the pilot, because it was "too cerebral" and lacking in action and adventure. They also objected to a female second-in-command—and to the guy with the pointed ears, saying that his demonic appearance might offend religious groups. However, they liked "The Cage" enough to do an unheard-of thing: ask for a second pilot.

Roddenberry brought in veteran writer Sam Peeples to provide the action-filled script for "Where No Man Has Gone Before," and started to work on revamping the series. Jeffrey Hunter chose not to continue in the role of Pike, so Canadian-born actor William Shatner was eventually cast in his place, and the captain was given a new name: James T. Kirk.

Shatner had appeared in film (*The Brothers Karamazov*), television, and on stage, in *The World of Suzie Wong*. Two years earlier, he had played another heroic lead in an unsold pilot, "Alexander the Great," which he playfully describes as " 'Combat' in drag." But his role as Alexander definitely influenced his portrayal of Kirk. In contrast to Jeffrey Hunter's brooding, somber performance as Pike, Shatner brought a warmth and likability to the role of the *Enterprise* captain. (In an interesting coincidence, Shatner had worked with Nimoy before, in a 1964 "Man from U.N.C.L.E." episode.) His initial impression, when Roddenberry showed him "The Cage," was that "it was a very imaginative and vital idea. . . . Then a script was written [for the second pilot], and I made some suggestions that Gene kindly said some time after had some import. . . . My general impressions were that it was a wonderful, vital idea that needed little change."

Lieutenant Commander Gary Mitchell (Gary Lockwood) and Dr. Elizabeth Dehner (Sally Kellerman) enjoy their newfound godhood in "Where No Man Has Gone Before." The contact lenses left the actors half-blind.

A phaser rifle–toting Kirk attempts to reason with Dr. Dehner

Despite NBC's request, Roddenberry was determined to keep the alien, Spock. He yielded to the request to drop the character of Number One, because, as he said, "It seemed to me that we were having so many arguments at this time that I couldn't save both of them, and so I decided to save the alien character. And it was at this time that we gave Mr. Spock the woman's logical unemotional qualities and kept him on the show. I then married the woman, but obviously, I could not have legally done it the other way round."

Spock was the only character from the first pilot to appear in the second. John Hoyt, who had played Dr. Phillip Boyce, was involved in other projects, so actor Paul Fix was cast as Dr. Piper. Guest stars Sally Kellerman and Gary Lockwood (the title character on "The Lieutenant") were cast as psychiatrist Elizabeth Dehner and crewman Gary Mitchell.

Despite network pressure to have an all-white crew, Roddenberry was determined that minorities should be represented on the *Enterprise*. Black actor Lloyd Haynes (best known as star of "Room 222") was cast as Lieutenant Alden, and George Takei as the Japanese-Filipino officer, Sulu. According to Takei (whose name rhymes with "okay"), "I think it was Gene's vision to have the makeup of the crew reflect the pluralism of this global society. I think Gene has often said, 'The *Starship Enterprise* was the Starship Earth in microcosm.'" Takei came away from his first meeting with Roddenberry convinced that he wouldn't get the role. He explains, "[Roddenberry] came out from behind his desk, and ushered me to a corner of his office where there was a coffee-table-and-couch-type setting, so it was a relaxed, comfortable setting rather than a formal test with a supplicant chair. It was really a very unusual interview, one on one, and we talked about

Leonard Nimoy as Mr. Spock, who is armed and ready for action in front of the shuttlecraft *Galileo*

Creating a Legend

What does it take to create one of the most enduringly popular characters in science fiction? Luck, genius, or a bit of both?

As Leonard Nimoy says, "It is a combination of talents. Writing, directing, acting. But even with those elements present, there is no guarantee the magic will take place."

But take place it did, with the character of Spock. From the very beginning, Gene Roddenberry knew that he wanted an alien in his science-fiction series, and that he wanted Leonard Nimoy to portray that alien. Said Roddenberry, "I made [Spock] a half-caste, because I remember thinking a half-breed Indian would be a lot more interesting than a full-blooded Indian or white, because he's going to be tugged in many directions."

But the character's alien background had yet to be fleshed out. In the first pilot (and some of the earliest episodes), Spock can be clearly seen emoting. However, when the character Number One was discarded along with the first pilot, Spock took on her trait of non-emotion, and the magic began to happen.

"What immediately intrigued me," Nimoy says, "was that here was a character who had an internal conflict. This half-human, half-Vulcan being, struggling to maintain a Vulcan attitude, a Vulcan philosophical posture and Vulcan logic, opposing what was fighting him internally, which was human emotion. There was a dynamic there to work with from an acting point of view."

Nimoy was suddenly faced with a number of creative choices; how does one show that internal conflict if the character *doesn't* express emotion? In his book *I Am Not Spock*, he describes how the Genesis of Spock was influenced by singer Harry Belafonte's performance at Los Angeles's Greek Theatre during the 1950s:

"During the first forty-five minutes of [Belafonte's] program he stood perfectly still at a center stage microphone, his shoulders slightly hunched, his hands resting on the front of his thighs. He simply sang. Then in the middle of a phrase, he finally made a move. He simply raised his right arm slowly until it was parallel to the floor . . . Had he been moving constantly, the gesture would have meant nothing. But following that long period of containment it was as though a cannonball had been fired.

"I found this idea very useful in Spock. When a stone face lifts an eyebrow, something has happened."

After a time, Nimoy came to know the character intimately— so intimately, in fact, that it began to affect him personally. He says, "It was helpful in making me see things more precisely and dispassionately; to get an objective view of the situation. What I didn't realize was the pressure cooker it put me into because I was, in character, suppressing my emotions. Once I'd got [the Spock makeup] all on, it was the strangest thing. I saw it happening in the mirror. It was as though, if I fooled around or laughed a lot, my face would crack. As though I would damage myself in some way; destroy the character and hurt myself. So I would just sit around and the rest of the cast would be fooling around, telling jokes or whatever, and I would just sit there, impassive. I would be enjoying myself but I wouldn't express it."

Leonard Nimoy and Gene Roddenberry share a lighthearted moment on set of the first pilot

Yet Nimoy's intimate knowledge of the character paid off, not only in his portrayal, but in other additions to STAR TREK lore. Certainly it was the reason the Spock neck pinch was created. The script "The Enemy Within" called for the Vulcan to steal up behind Kirk's evil alter ego and knock him out with the butt of a phaser.

Nimoy found the idea incompatible with Spock's pacifistic Vulcan philosophy, so he suggested to the director that Vulcans had studied human anatomy and developed a less violent method of rendering recalcitrant humans unconscious. The director asked for a demonstration. Nimoy "explained to Bill Shatner what I had in mind and when I applied the pressure at the proper point, Bill stiffened and dropped in a heap. That's how the Vulcan neck pinch was born."

Nimoy used his Jewish upbringing in creating the Vulcan hand salute, first used in the episode "Amok Time." The salute derived from that used by the Kohanim, Hebrew priests, when blessing the congregation while forming the letter *shin* with their hands. The gesture is now used as a greeting by STAR TREK fans everywhere.

Kirk and McCoy (DeForest
Kelley) in an early publicity shot

barking dog by shooting it—a far cry from that lovable curmudgeon Dr. McCoy). But Roddenberry eventually convinced the network otherwise and, as soon as the actor became available, cast him as Leonard "Bones" McCoy. Interestingly, Kelley had worked with Leonard Nimoy before, in an episode of "The Virginian." He recalls laughingly, "[Nimoy] later reminded me of that . . . [I played a] drunken doctor and I let him die."

Roddenberry also cast Nichelle Nichols in the role of Lieutenant Uhura ("*uhuru*" means "freedom" in Swahili). Nichols's first dramatic television experience had come three years earlier, when she had appeared in an episode of "The Lieutenant." She was singing in England when her agent contacted her about the possibility of a role in a new science-fiction series; she was enjoying her stay in Europe and refused at first to return to the States. But her agent persisted, and finally convinced her by paying for a plane ticket

The world's most popular alien . . .

. . . and his beloved nemesis, "Bones" McCoy, as photographed by Gene Trindl in 1967

Making a Difference

As "STAR TREK" developed, Nichelle Nichols's frustration grew. While preliminary script drafts might show her character, Uhura, having a significant scene or two in the episode, final drafts invariably cut her contribution to "Hailing frequencies open, Captain." Finally, in desperation, she confronted Roddenberry, and when no satisfactory response came, she quit.

This occurred on a Friday. That night, Nichols chanced to attend an NAACP fund-raiser—and one of the attendees just happened to be Dr. Martin Luther King.

King, it turned out, was a fan of the show, and asked to be introduced to Nichols. When she confessed that she was leaving the series, King strongly urged her to remain, as her character served as a role model not only for blacks, but for everyone.

Because of his words, Nichols returned to the show, and later told Hugh Downs in a "20/20" interview, "I knew that now black children must look at me on that ship even if I was just pushing some buttons and know that 'this is a person I can identify with, that I can emulate.'"

One of those kids was Whoopi Goldberg, who told *Starlog* magazine, "I've been a Trekkie from way back. The only time you ever saw black people in the future was on STAR TREK."

Guinan and her role model: Whoopi Goldberg and Nichelle Nichols share a hug on the ST:TNG set

When Goldberg contacted the producers of ST:TNG and asked to be included in the series, they tried to politely decline. Gene Roddenberry assumed that a star of Goldberg's magnitude would insist on a leading role, but when he spoke with her, he learned otherwise.

"She said, 'No, you don't get it, do you? What I am saying is that I love STAR TREK. It's been close to my mind all my adult life and I want to play a part in the new series even if I just sweep the floor. I don't want to be the star of it. I don't want to deprive anyone of their job. I just want to be a part of what this is doing for people.' She had been affected by *The Original Series* and she understood, perhaps more than many, what drama could do for people."

Thus the character of Guinan, the hostess of Ten-Forward, was born, thanks at least in part to Nichols's decision to remain with *The Original Series*.

Mr. Spock and Lieutenant Uhura (Nichelle Nichols) take care of business on the bridge

home. When Nichols went in to read for STAR TREK, there was no part in the script for her, so she read for the part of Spock. "We did a nice long reading, a scene that was several pages long," she recalls, "and when I finished, one of the guys said, 'Call down to personnel to see if Leonard Nimoy has signed his contract yet!'"

Grace Lee Whitney, who had appeared in the films *Top Banana* and *Some Like It Hot,* was hired to replace Andrea Dromm as the captain's yeoman. (Whitney had also appeared in Roddenberry's "Police Story" pilot with De Kelley.) Majel Barrett returned to the show in a different guise—that of Nurse Christine Chapel. NBC executives had not liked Barrett's portrayal of Number One, so Barrett came up with a plan: she bleached her hair blond and went into Roddenberry's office.

Kirk and "Charlie X" (Robert Walker, Jr.) prepare for a workout in the *Enterprise* gymnasium

"I sat there talking to his secretary, Penny, and Gene walked in. He looked at me and at Penny, said, 'Good morning,' and walked in the door. . . . I kept on talking to Penny, and pretty soon Gene came out again, put some papers on Penny's desk, sort of smiled at me, turned around, and walked back in his office. Then the double take happened. He opened the door and said, 'Majel?!' And I said, 'By God, if I could fool you, I can fool NBC.'"

With characters in place, STAR TREK went into series production, at a cost to NBC of $180,000 per episode. By August of 1966, Roddenberry had settled into the role of executive producer, with Gene L. Coon as producer and Robert H. Justman as associate producer.

In September 1966, Roddenberry decided to garner a little advance publicity by showing the pilot "Where No Man" to attendees of the World

The *Enterprise* landing party beams into an apparently deserted (and amazingly Earthlike) city in "Miri"

Science Fiction Convention in Cleveland. Understandably nervous about audience reaction as his show began, Roddenberry snapped at a "rather loud gentleman" to be quiet. "And Isaac Asimov said, 'Yes, you're perfectly right. We will tone it down.' And someone said, 'You're dead, you just insulted Isaac Asimov.'" As it turned out, Asimov took no offense; in fact, he became an enthusiastic supporter of the show who often corresponded with Roddenberry.

The audience's reaction? A standing ovation.

STAR TREK made its television debut on Thursday, September 8, 1966, at 8:30 P.M. For the most part, reviews were less than generous. Said *Variety:*

STAR TREK obviously solicits all-out suspension of disbelief, but it won't work. Even within its sci-fi frame of reference it was an incredible and dreary mess of confusion and complexities at the kickoff. . . . By a generous stretch of the imagination, it could lure a small coterie of the smallfry, though not happily time slotted in that direction. It's better suited to the Saturday morning kidvid bloc . . .

However, Nielsen ratings reveal that it actually outpulled its competition—for that week, at least. A curious phenomenon began to occur: as the series' ratings began a slow decline, its fan mail began to increase. According to Dorothy Fontana, "The first week after the show was on, a sack of mail began arriving, and I said, 'That's nice, that's really good.' And the second week, five sacks of mail came in. After that, they became so heavy we couldn't deal with it anymore."

The episode that really drew the fans was John D. F. Black's "The Naked Time," which brought the series' characters to life by revealing their innermost selves. Infected by a disease that causes one's hidden side to surface, Kirk mourns the fact that his devotion to his ship requires the sacrifice of a more human brand of love. Sulu brandishes a sword à la D'Artagnan and Nurse Chapel pines over a certain Vulcan, while Spock weeps over his inability to tell his mother he loves her. Said Leonard Nimoy, "I like to think that the episode led our

Captain Kirk comes dangerously close to a fatal encounter with "Nancy Crater" (Jeanne Bal), aka "the salt vampire" in "The Man Trap," the first STAR TREK episode aired

Costumes by William Ware Theiss

So how in the puritanical 1960s, when a mere navel or the underside of a breast was enough to send network censors reeling, did STAR TREK's costume designer, the late Bill Theiss, manage to get away with so . . . little?

True, Theiss put *The Original Series'* crewwomen into ultra-short skirts well in advance of that decade's mini craze. And true, the female guest stars were clad in Theiss's beautiful—but undeniably alluring—creations.

Yet Theiss insisted that it was not necessarily the *amount* of skin shown that made the costumes seem extraordinarily revealing, but rather the manner in which that skin was shown. Hence the "Theiss Titillation Theory": The degree to which an outfit seems sexy is directly proportional to the degree it appears to be on the verge of slipping off.

Certainly, the theory applied to Leslie Parrish's pink chiffon Greek gown in "Who Mourns for Adonais?" It consisted of a fitted piece of chiffon that covered Leslie's bosom and was anchored solely at one point on the long, flowing skirt, and by the weight of fabric draped over one shoulder. Leslie reported that the costume was perfectly comfortable, and that she was not at all nervous about wearing it—while those around her reported exactly the opposite reaction.

The Titillation Theory had a corollary: Bareness in unexpected places. Said Theiss, "The costumes were designed to be bare in places that you normally weren't used to seeing bare skin. For the most part, they were not any more or less bare, or more or less structurally unsound. There were a few things that were very fragile, like in 'Elaan of Troyius,' that silver on black mesh thing that was constantly being sewed on the set because the mesh was so fragile. But that was done to utilize that particular fabric in that situation.

"I always tried to start out with what was appropriate for the script and the character . . . and what Gene liked." He always considered whether the clothing was suitable for the "planet of the week." And while in theory he designed for the future, he always kept in mind that the costumes also had to be acceptable to today's viewing audience.

When Roddenberry began putting together STAR TREK: THE NEXT GENERATION, he immediately recruited Theiss. In designing the new Starfleet uniforms, Theiss created another stir by putting a spin on the old miniskirt idea with the "scant," a short tunic worn by some of the *Enterprise*'s male

Costumer Bill Theiss adjusting one of his creations for Susan Oliver

crew members. The scant appeared mainly in first-season episodes.

A native of Boston, Theiss graduated from Stanford with a degree in design and landed a job as an artist in Universal's advertising department. From there, he moved on to CBS Television City, where he served as costumer for two soap operas. His television credits include "The Donna Reed Show," "The Dick Van Dyke Show," "My Favorite Martian," and "General Hospital," as well as two pilots for Gene Roddenberry—"Genesis II" and "Planet Earth." Theiss was nominated three times for an Oscar—*Bound for Glory* (1976), *Butch and Sundance: The Early Days* (1979), and *Heart Like a Wheel* (1983)—and won an Emmy for his costume designs on STAR TREK: THE NEXT GENERATION.

The Theiss Titillation Theory in Action: (Clockwise, from right) Lieutenant Carolyn Palamas (Leslie Parrish) and her seemingly precarious Greek gown in "Who Mourns for Adonais?"; Angelique Pettyjohn as drill thrall Shahna in "The Gamesters of Triskelion"; and Susan Oliver as the infamous green Orion slave woman

A Fuzzy Thing Happened on the Way to Antares

One of the most appealing aspects of STAR TREK was its occasional indulgence in lighthearted humor, and one of the persons to thank for that is William Shatner, who recalls:

"I got a call from Gene Roddenberry, who said he had made a science-fiction pilot called STAR TREK which hadn't sold, and would I come back to Hollywood to see if I wanted to play the lead in a second pilot? So I went back to Hollywood and saw this pilot. It had a lot of wonderful things in it. But I also saw that the people in it were playing it as though 'We're out in space, isn't this serious?' I thought if it was a naval vessel at sea, they'd be relaxed and familiar, not somewhat pedantic and self-important about being out in space. It seemed to me that they wouldn't be so serious about it. And the fact that I had come off all these years in comedy—I wanted it to be lighter rather than heavier. So I consciously thought of playing good-pal-the-captain, who, in time of need, would snap to and become the warrior. I broached this idea to Gene, and it seemed to strike a note."

Dorothy Fontana, STAR TREK story editor, comments on the development of humor in the series: "The show was pretty straightforward in the beginning, but then we realized that any time we'd give the characters something humorous to play with, the show really sparked. . . . We began to see the opportunities for humor in a lot of the interpersonal reactions and interchanges between characters . . . for example, this is probably just about the time where Bones starts bickering with Spock."

Leonard Nimoy said of the McCoy/Spock verbal fencing, "I always tried to play these scenes very dry . . . in all these arguments, I always modeled Spock after George Burns and his cigar. George's rather bemused, unflustered acceptance of Gracie's ramblings really influenced Spock's interaction with McCoy."

Shatner also credits writer/producer Gene Coon with injecting humor into the scripts. It was Coon who cowrote "A Piece of the Action," in which Kirk serves as inept chauffeur of a 1920s "flivver," and Coon who donated the infamous "my friend got his ears caught in a ricepicker" line in "The City on the Edge of Forever."

One of the most popular humorous episodes was "The Trouble with Tribbles," written by David

Cheese it, it's "Da Feds": Spock and "Da Big Boss" in "A Piece of the Action"

Gerrold, who was nineteen at the time he sold the episode. (His original title was "A Fuzzy Thing Happened to Me.") Says he, "I don't write humor. I write serious stories about people who are very funny. When you look at Kirk and Spock and the others, these are the best and brightest in Starfleet. They're very intelligent people. They're not above playfulness and teasing and gentle jokes at each other's expense. And I think that demonstrates how much they love each other. . . . This show was blessed with three great comedians. William Shatner can deliver the most atrocious jokes with an absolute straight face . . . Leonard Nimoy is absolutely hysterical by being the 'great stone face.' And De Kelley, by raising his eyebrow, can be as funny as Jack Benny doing the great sideways stare. How could you not write 'funny' for these three great comedians?"

Say Goodnight, Gracie: Spock directs a disdainful brow at an indignant Dr. McCoy

**Science Officer Spock at his
station on the bridge**

audience to understand that inside Mr. Spock's cool exterior there was
something sensitive and vulnerable. It might be a coincidence, but within
a few days after that episode went on the air, my fan mail jumped from
dozens of pieces per week to thousands."

Indeed, the STAR TREK characters had become immensely popular—
especially the guy with the pointed ears. None of them anticipated the
overwhelming audience reaction; as Nimoy says, "I had no idea. No inkling
at all. I didn't even bother to take my phone number out of the book. After
the show went on the air people started to call me up. It took a while for me
to realize that I was going to have to make some changes in my lifestyle. . . . I can't emphasize how great the shock was."

Apparently NBC had no inkling, either, when it arranged for Nimoy to
be Grand Marshal of the annual Pear Blossom Festival in Medford, Oregon.
The parade went as planned, but when the crowd learned that Nimoy would

sign autographs, chaos ensued. Traffic was brought to a standstill, and Nimoy "escaped" only with the help of local police.

According to William Shatner's memoirs *Star Trek Memories*, Nimoy's escalating popularity began to bother Shatner, who freely admits that he was troubled by the realization that he was no longer the only star of the show. When Shatner voiced his concerns to Roddenberry, the producer responded, "Don't ever fear having good and popular people around you, because they can only enhance your own performance." Roddenberry discussed this problem in his correspondence with Isaac Asimov, who suggested that the close friendship between Kirk and Spock be emphasized on the show. That way, when viewers thought of Spock, they would naturally think of the captain as well. The advice worked.

Extremely rare photos of Shatner and Nimoy taken by photographer Ken Whitmore

Yet the STAR TREK characters' incredible popularity with their fans failed to be reflected in the Nielsen ratings. By the end of 1966, NBC let it be known that it was unhappy with the ratings—and considering canceling the show.

Science-fiction writer Harlan Ellison, who was then working on a STAR TREK episode, spearheaded the first "Save STAR TREK" letter-writing campaign. He sent out five thousand letters from "The Committee," a group of science-fiction notables that included Ellison, Robert Bloch, Theodore Sturgeon, Poul Anderson, Lester Del Rey, and Philip José Farmer. The letters urged series fans to write NBC protesting STAR TREK's cancellation.

Apparently, NBC was impressed with the response: the show was renewed for a second season. In the meantime, some of the finest first-season episodes aired, among them Paul Schneider's "Balance of Terror." The episode dealt with prejudice, turning the Federation's formerly faceless enemy, the Romulans, into noble, eloquent beings, one of whom tells Kirk, "In another reality, I might have called you 'friend.'"

That line was delivered by actor Mark Lenard, who would go on to become famous as Mr. Spock's father in STAR TREK's second season. The Romulan commander was Lenard's first television role; he had arrived in Hollywood just three weeks earlier.

Arguably the finest STAR TREK episode is "The City on the Edge of Forever," by Harlan Ellison. The story is classic tragedy: Kirk must stand by and watch the woman he loves (played by Joan Collins) die so that history will remain unaltered. However, Roddenberry massively rewrote the original

Hollywood newcomer Mark Lenard (right) as the Romulan commander in "Balance of Terror"

A heartbroken Kirk permits the woman he loves to die in "City on the Edge of Forever"

script, much to Ellison's consternation. In an interview with Tom Snyder on the *Tomorrow* program, Ellison commented, ". . . they had mucked it up badly. It took six or seven years before Gene Roddenberry and I even spoke to each other again. . . ."

Writer Sam Peeples concurred. "I thought [Harlan's] version of his script that won the Writer's Guild Award was far better than the script that was shot. . . . [but] When you produce a series there are circumstances—hundreds of reasons why you may have to change a script. The original writer of that script is not aware of these, and even if you tell him he doesn't necessarily believe you because he likes what he did. . . ."

According to Roddenberry, "Harlan . . . wrote a $350,000 estimated budget show when I only had, in those days, $186,000. . . . He then submitted it to the Writer's Guild, which gave him the Writer's Guild prize. . . . I rewrote that script for Harlan, and it won the Nebula Award, which he rushed up on stage and took credit for, too!"

At the beginning of the second season, a new character, Ensign Pavel Chekov, joined the *Enterprise* crew. According to the network's press release, Chekov was added because *Pravda* had complained about the fact that no Russians were represented on the show. However, actor Walter Koenig, who portrayed the young ensign, has a different take:

"Well, the facts are that they were looking for somebody who would appeal to the bubblegum set. They had somebody in mind like Davey Jones of 'The Monkees,' and originally it was supposed to be an English character . . . however, in acknowledgment of the Russians' contribution to space they made the decision to go that way."

Kirk, McCoy, and Spock before the Guardian of Forever after their return from 1930s Earth

STAR TREK's "Other Gene"

The late Gene L. Coon joined the "Star Trek" staff in mid-first season to serve as writer-producer (a "hyphenate," in the TV industry parlance). The multitalented Coon had also freelanced for television shows like "Dragnet," "Bonanza," and "Wagon Train," as well as numerous others. He came to STAR TREK from a stint on "The Wild, Wild West" and later would go on to help create "The Munsters."

Coon brought welcome relief for Roddenberry, who was already exhausted from the strain of producing a weekly series. "By the time Gene Coon came on board," recalls original series producer Bob Justman, "Gene Roddenberry's physical stamina was about gone." Justman remembers Coon as speaking "in this odd, dry, clipped manner. He looked like a Methodist preacher from Arkansas"—in fact, Coon hailed from Nebraska. "Or a banker who's just about to foreclose on you. [When I first met him] I thought he was one cold, hard, mean son of a bitch. That was my physical impression of him. It didn't take long before I realized that Gene Coon, in addition to his enormous writing abilities, was a wonderfully warm, sensitive, generous, sweet, decent person. He was a phenomenon. I've seen people write before, but I've never seen anyone who could, when a script needed to be written, sit down in two days and not only knock out a script, but the script would be twenty or thirty pages too long. He was a machine gun. He was terrific."

Roddenberry agreed: "I found him to be an immensely inventive writer and immensely devoted to many of the things that I was devoted to. He had the ability to write fast and well. I remember once he did a forty-two-page memo on a thirty-eight-page script. We worked together on many things over the years. It was great fun. I loved him."

William Shatner notes that Gene Coon's arrival was soon followed by a noticeable improvement in later first-season scripts (among them "Devil in the Dark," "Errand of Mercy," and "Space Seed," all fully or partially credited to Coon).

The Prime Directive, the Organian Peace Treaty, and the series' favorite villains, the Klingons, all sprang from Coon's creative mind. He also had a talent for bringing characters to life; he helped develop the friendly feud between Dr. McCoy and Mr. Spock, and the characterization of Engineer Scott as a "complaining miracle worker."

Gene Coon at his typewriter

Coon's writing habits were as unique as his scripts. Every time he got mired down in a story problem, he simply went to sleep. By morning, when he woke, the solution always presented itself, and he would write at a frenetic—but never sloppy—pace until lunchtime, then take the rest of the day off.

During STAR TREK's three-year run, Coon also contributed to the episodes "Arena," "Metamorphosis," "Who Mourns for Adonais?," "The Apple," "Bread and Circuses," and "A Piece of the Action." He left as series producer during the second season to work on "The Name of the Game," though he wrote the third-year episode "Spectre of the Gun" under the pseudonym Lee Cronin.

Sadly, Coon died of lung cancer in 1973, before the series' "renaissance" and the advent of STAR TREK conventions; as a result, he was never interviewed as were others who worked on the show, and his great contribution to STAR TREK remains largely unsung.

Lieutenant Sulu (George Takei) at the helm, flanked by Ensign Pavel Chekov (Walter Koenig)

The Russian accent comes naturally to Koenig, whose father hailed from Lithuania and spoke Russian at home.

In the meantime, NBC had changed its mind about keeping Spock well in the background; because of the character's enormous popularity, the new network VP encouraged Roddenberry to focus more on the Vulcan. After all, it was becoming pretty clear that Spock's satanic good looks and Leonard Nimoy's ability to convey great depth of repressed emotion with the merest lift of an eyebrow struck a lot of female viewers as . . . well, sexy.

Said Nimoy, "The first indication [of Spock's sex appeal] was when a lovely actress visited the set with my agent. I was in costume with all the makeup on when we were introduced. She said, 'Oh, God, can I touch your ears?' It's a silly thing to say, I know, but she was serious. She really wanted to touch them."

It's no secret that most Vulcanophiles are women. Just what is the secret of Vulcan appeal?

"Something exciting about the devilish eyes and ears," Nimoy postulates. "A character who could not express emotions and, therefore, could not express love. That could express a challenge to a lady who believes she may be the one to teach him about love."

Whatever the secret, the Vulcans remain one of the most popular alien races in science-fiction history. As a consequence of growing interest in "Vulcanalia," the season's premiere was "Amok Time," which gave the viewing audience its first and only glimpse of Spock's home planet. Spock's already-established greater strength and keener hearing helped the STAR TREK staff work backward in establishing the planet's characteristics—greater gravity, thinner atmosphere. Writer Theodore Sturgeon certainly also understood about Vulcan sex appeal, for he introduced the *pon farr*, the Vulcan seven-year mating cycle. The episode also marked the first use of the Vulcan hand salute (which posed quite a challenge for guest actress Celia Lovsky, who played the matriarch T'Pau) and the now-famous greeting, "Live long and prosper."

All of Vulcan rolled into one package: The matriarch, T'Pau (Celia Lovsky)

T'Pring (Arlene Martel) stops a disgruntled Spock from ringing her chime

Another second-season "Vulcan" episode was "Journey to Babel," which introduced Spock's parents, the human Amanda and the Vulcan ambassador Sarek, and dealt with the eighteen-year rift between father and son. The episode was written by story editor D. C. (Dorothy) Fontana, one of the series' finest writers. Fontana's

Mr. Spock Is Dreamy!

*The not-quite-human thinking machines may be starting
a new trend in sex appeal*

An Essay by Isaac Asimov

(This piece first appeared in "TV Guide," April 29, 1967.)

A revolution of incalculable importance may be sweeping America, thanks to television. And thanks particularly to STAR TREK, which, in its noble and successful effort to present good science fiction to the American public, has also presented everyone with an astonishing revelation.

I was put onto the matter by my blonde, blue-eyed, and beautiful daughter, who is just turning twelve and who, in all the practical matters that count, is more clear-sighted than I.

It happened one evening when we were watching STAR TREK together and holding our breath while Captain Kirk and Mr. Spock faced a menace of overwhelming proportions.

Captain Kirk (for those, if any, who are not STAR TREK fans) is a capable hero and a full-blooded human. Mr. Spock is half-alien and is a creature of pure reason and no emotion. Naturally Captain Kirk responded to every danger with an appropriate twist of his handsome and expressive face. Spock, however, kept his long, serene face unmoved. Not for an instant did he allow emotion to dim the thoughtful gleam of his eye; not for a split second did he allow that long face to grow shorter.

And my daughter said, "I think Mr. Spock is *dreamy!*"

I started! If my daughter said Mr. Spock was dreamy, then he was dreamy to the entire feminine population of the world, for my daughter is plugged into that vague something called "femininity" and her responses are infallible.

But how could that be? Mr. Spock dreamy? He had a strong face, of course, but it was so solemn and serious, so cool; his eyebrows were drawn so outward and upward, and his large ears came to such a long, sharp upper point.

How could he compare with full-blooded Earthlings with normal ears and eyebrows, who were suave, sophisticated, and devilishly handsome to boot? Like me, for instance, just to pick an example at random.

"Why is he dreamy?" I asked my daughter.

"Because," she said, "he's so *smart!*"

There's no doubt about it. I have asked other girls and they agree. Through the agency of Mr. Spock, STAR TREK has been capitalizing upon a fact not generally known among the male half of the population.

Women think being smart is sexy!

A smart
(and secretly
sensitive) guy

Do you know what this means to me? Can you imagine what a load of guilt it has taken off my back? Can you imagine what a much greater load of vain regret it has put on my back?

But, heaven help me, it wasn't my fault. I was misled. When I was young I read books about children; books for which *Tom Sawyer* was the prototype. Anyone else old enough to remember those books?

Remember the kid hero? Wasn't he a delightful little chap? Wasn't he manly? He played hooky all the time and went swimming at the old swimming hole. Remember? He never knew his lessons; he swiped apples; he used bad grammar and threw rocks at cats. *You* remember.

And do you remember that little sneaky kid we all hated so? He was an unbearable wretch who wore clean clothes, and did his lessons, and got high marks, and spoke like a dude. All the kids hated him, and so did all the readers. Rotten little smart kid!

As I read such stories, I realized that because I had known no better I had unwittingly been committing the terrible sin of doing well at school. Oh, I did my best to change and follow the paths of rectitude and virtue, and dip girls' pigtails in inkwells and draw nasty pictures of the teacher on my slate, and steal a pumpkin—but girls didn't have pigtails and I didn't have a slate and nobody I knew across the length and breadth of Brooklyn's slums had any idea of what a pumpkin was.

And when the teacher would ask a question, I would, quite automatically and without thinking, give the right answer—and there I would be. Sunk in vice again! Talk about a monkey on your back!

There was no way out. By the time I was in high school I realized I was rotten clean through and all I could do was hope the FBI never saw my report card.

Then, somewhere late in high school, I became aware of an even more serious difficulty!

I had been noticing for a while that girls didn't look quite as awful as I had earlier thought. I was even speculating that there might be some purpose in wasting some time in speaking to one or two of them, if I could figure out how one went about it.

I decided the place to learn was the movies, since these often concerned themselves with this very problem.

Remember those movie heroes? Strong, solemn, and with a vocabulary of ten easy words and fifteen grunts? And remember the key sentence in every one of those pictures?

You don't? Well, I'll tell you. Some girl is interested in the movie hero. She sees something in him she does not see in any other character in the film, and I was keenly intent on finding what that something might be.

To be sure, the hero was taller and stronger and handsomer and better dressed than any other male in the picture, but surely this was purely superficial. No female would be in the least attracted to such mere surface characteristics. There had to be something deep and hidden, and I recognized what this might be in that key sentence I mentioned.

The woman says to her girl friend, "I love that big lug!" Or sometimes she says to the hero himself, "I love you, you big lug!"

That was it! Hollywood was of the definite opinion that for a man to be attractive to women he had to be a big lug. I ran to Webster's (second edition) to look up the word and found no less than eight definitions. Definition number eight was: "A heavy or clumsy lout; a blockhead."

It was school all over again. I could manage being clumsy but I could never keep up that blockhead business long. I'd be doing fine for a while, glazing my eyes, and remembering to say "Duh" when spoken to. But, sooner or later, at some unguarded moment, I would say something rational, and bitter shame would overcome me. It was no use; I could never attain that glorious lughood that would have put me at ease with women.

T'Pring and the Vulcan she left at the altar

I got married at last, somehow. My theory is that the young lady who married me must have seen that under my suave man-of-the-world exterior, there was a lout and a blockhead striving for expression. So she married me for inner beauty.

Then came television. Remember the husbands in the situation comedies? Stupid, right? Have you ever seen one who could tie his shoes without help? Have you ever seen one smart enough to put anything over on his wife? Or on his five-year-old niece for that matter?

That was one thing all situation comedies had in common—the stupidity of the husband. The other things were the smartness of the wife and the depth of her love for her husband.

These points can't be unconnected, can they? Anyone can see that the only deduction to draw from this is that wives, being smart, love their husbands *because* they are stupid.

All I can say is that for years and years I have done my best to be a stupid husband. My wife, loyal creature that she is, has assured me over and over again that I have succeeded beyond my wildest dreams and that I am the stupidest husband who ever lived. She seems so sincere when she says it, and yet I have always had to ask: Is it merely her kind heart speaking? Can she be just flattering me?

And then, *then*, came this blinding revelation. Here I had been watching STAR TREK since its inception because I like it, because it is well done, because it is exciting, because it says things (subtly and neatly) that are difficult to say in "straight" drama, and because science fiction, properly presented, is the type of literature most appropriate to our generation.

But it hadn't occurred to me that Mr. Spock was sexy. I had never realized that such a thing was possible; that girls palpitate over the way one eyebrow goes up a fraction; that they squeal with passion when a little smile quirks his lip. And all because he's *smart!*

If I had only known! If I had only known!

But I am spreading the word now. It may be far too late for me (well, almost), but there is a new generation to consider!

Men! Men everywhere! Don't list to the lies! I have learned the secret at last. It is sexy to be smart!

Do you hear me, men? Relax and be your natural selves! Stop aiming at lughood. *It's sexy to be smart!*

Just one thing bothers me. Can it be Mr. Spock's ears? Webster's (second edition) gives that blockhead definition as its eighth. Its definition number two for that same word is "ear."

Could it be that when a girl says, "I love you, you big lug," she means the man's ears are as big as Mr. Spock's?

Well, just in case, while I'm being smart, I'll also let my ears grow.

"Journey to Babel": McCoy chats with Spock's parents, Amanda (Jane Wyatt) and Ambassador Sarek (Mark Lenard)

scripts did much to develop the background of Spock, who she freely admits was her favorite STAR TREK character.

A veteran writer who had already sold nine television scripts, Fontana first came to work for STAR TREK in a secretarial position, but continued to freelance. During the show's first season, she wrote the episodes "Charlie X" and "Tomorrow Is Yesterday." Her talent so impressed Roddenberry that, near the end of the first season, as she recalls, "[he] called me and asked, '. . . Would you like to try [being] story editor?' And I said yes. He gave me a major rewrite to do. If I could do the rewrite on time and to the satisfaction of both the studio and the network, then I could be a story editor."

The rewrite was on Nathan Butler's [Jerry Sohl's pseudonym] script for "The Way of the Spores," which in Fontana's hands became "This Side of Paradise." According to Fontana, "The story started out being a love story for Sulu, and it really wasn't working. That's why Leila Kalomi was named as she was. I'm sure that they assumed it would be someone like a Hawaiian-type girl. It just wasn't working because there were a lot of problems with it. I went in to Gene and said, 'You know what's wrong with this story? It should be a Spock love story.' And he thought about that for a while and said, 'Okay. Write that.' . . .

"I had to do a complete and total rewrite . . . restructuring the story and changing the characters. Now it became Spock, and if Spock is affected, how does that change the relationships to the rest of the crew? If he can feel emotion, suddenly he's somebody they don't know. It was nice to have fun with it, because Leonard could sense the inherent ability to carry that off . . . now he's free, suddenly—he can do other things. And that was very liberating; that was fun."

Fontana went on to write some of the series' best episodes, including "Friday's Child," "By Any Other Name," "The Ultimate Computer," and "The *Enterprise* Incident."

In the middle of the second season, NBC again hinted that STAR TREK might be headed for cancellation. However, this time it wasn't a science-fiction writer who spearheaded the "Save STAR TREK" letter-

An evil, knife-brandishing alter-Sulu

(*Below left*) Scott, McCoy, Kirk, and Uhura find themselves in a hostile alternate universe and midriff-revealing costumes in "Mirror, Mirror"
(*Below right*) A bearded alter-Spock invades McCoy's mind

The Woman Who Saved STAR TREK

All fans of STAR TREK owe a special debt to a certain lady named Bjo (pronounced BEE-jo) Trimble.

While Bjo is certainly a fan of the series, she can hardly be described as a "typical" fan. In fact, she first became involved with Gene Roddenberry before STAR TREK ever aired—at the 1966 World Science Fiction Convention, where Roddenberry was peddling his brand-new show. Roddenberry was determined to get a couple of the show's costumes into the convention's "futuristic fashion show" at the last minute—and Bjo, in charge of the event, was initially just as determined not to let him. But, as she reports, Roddenberry convinced her with his "Irish charm," and the encounter made her curious about the new television show.

Both she and her husband, John, became loyal fans, and were later invited onto the set of STAR TREK—during the second season, just as the cast learned of the series' cancellation.

Says Bjo: "It was very disheartening to watch, because people would go on and do their lines and be 'up' and cheerful members of the *Enterprise*. And then they'd come out and go 'Ugggh!' . . . It was really a sad thing.

"On the way home, John said these fatal words: 'There ought to be something we could do about this.' "

They did something, all right. Bjo went to the secretaries at Desilu and learned what it took for a letter to be noticed by the executives. She then procured the mailing lists for the three most recent World Science Fiction Conventions. All told, the Trimbles sent out between four and six thousand letters, all of them urging fans to write to the studio executives.

And the response?

The precise number of letters NBC received is difficult to pinpoint, as officially the network only admitted to sixty thousand. However, an unofficial source—a programmer hired by NBC to compile a demographic profile of STAR TREK fans—reported that a whopping one million letters were received by NBC.

The series was renewed for a third season. Had it not been, there would not have been enough episodes to permit syndication—and it was while the series was in rerun syndication that STAR TREK fandom mushroomed.

Bjo and John Trimble remained active in fandom, and, along with fans all over the country, organized STAR TREK conventions. Why did STAR TREK inspire such a loyal, vocal following? Says Bjo, "John and I were the ones answering the [STAR TREK fan] mail, living in a part of LA that was full of hippies. And what we saw was that STAR TREK was promising a future two hundred years from now. In the sixties, hands were hovering over red buttons; it was brinkmanship to the nth degree. People were saying, 'There's no tomorrow, so blow your little heads off with drugs today.' And all of a sudden, here are old-fashioned heroes, old-fashioned values in a future two hundred years from now with, my God, blacks and Orientals participating. It was kind of a galvanizing feeling. The show got people involved."

William Shatner (center) with extras Bjo Trimble (left) and writer David Gerrold (right) on the set of STAR TREK: THE MOTION PICTURE

writing campaign, but a science-fiction fan by the name of Bjo Trimble. With the help of her husband, John, Trimble organized a letter-writing campaign that buried NBC executives in a mountain of mail, all written by fans pleading for STAR TREK's renewal.

The overwhelmed network acquiesced, promising Roddenberry a 7:30 P.M. Monday night time slot. But the promise was broken—and STAR TREK was put in a 10 P.M. Friday night slot, one that guaranteed poor ratings and eventual cancellation. Frustrated, Roddenberry quit the show. Unfortunately, Gene Coon had gone to work for "The Name of the Game," and Dorothy Fontana left the staff to freelance. At the same time, the studio cut the show's budget.

The loss of funding and talent began to affect the show; the third-season premiere was "Spock's Brain," hardly the best the series had to offer. However, there were several excellent episodes, including "The *Enterprise* Incident," which provided another intriguing look at the Romu-lans, and "Is There in Truth No Beauty?," in which Diana Muldaur made her second guest-star appearance. The latter episode was notable for its mention of the IDIC philosophy— Infinite Diversity in Infinite Combina-tions, a celebration of our differences.

Of course, no mention of the third season would be complete without "Plato's Stepchildren,"

If I Only Had a Brain: Kirk confronts his witless first officer in "Spock's Brain"

One of the advantages Gene Roddenberry had producing "STAR TREK" was that he was able to tackle social issues that would never get past the 1960s network censors on a more down-to-Earth drama. In the great tradition of Jonathan Swift and *Gulliver's Travels*, Roddenberry and the many writers who contributed to the "STAR TREK" universe were able to attain a level of social commentary that was ahead of its time—all because the series used the trappings of the fantastic as a backdrop. "STAR TREK" stories became morality plays, sophisticated enough to hold up and maintain their relevance nearly thirty years later.

"STAR TREK"'s special spin—born of the volatile era in which it was conceived—was that these morality tales could encourage viewers to think along the lines of such then-radical liberal beliefs as "All men are equal, no matter what the color of their skin" and "No good comes of getting involved in other people's internal wars."

This was strong stuff in the sixties. Only undisciplined youths and the occasional daring politician were bold enough to make such statements in public. Certainly no network with sponsors to worry about was going to put up with a mainstream television program taking these positions.

So "STAR TREK" used its science-fiction guise to make the statements more palatable. The most obvious challenge to the status quo was the racially mixed nature of the crew of the *U.S.S. Enterprise*. With forced busing a pressing concern, it wouldn't have been advisable to state openly, "Starfleet doesn't care if a person is black or white or yellow—this is an equal-opportunity employer." So "STAR TREK" openly stated that all *species*, like Vulcans, for example, were allowed to serve in Starfleet, while implying that the same held for all human races by casting a variety of minorities in visible roles.

It was "STAR TREK" that in 1967 aired the controversial interracial kiss between Captain Kirk and Lieutenant Uhura, the first ever on television. This was dangerous ground when there was a real danger that some affiliate stations, especially in the "Bible Belt," would "black out" or refuse to air the episode because of the kiss. In the end, no one warned the station managers about the episode's radical content and the episode aired across the country without trouble.

A love-smitten and happy Mr. Spock with Leila Kalomi (Jill Ireland) in "This Side of Paradise"

Racial tolerance was also the subject of an entire episode, "Let That Be Your Last Battlefield," which portrayed two eternally warring species, one black on the right side and white on the left side, the other black on the left side and white on the right side. The episode wasn't subtle in its approach, but it dealt with racial tensions and their potential tragic results in a way that no "real life" drama could have hoped to do.

Although Roddenberry had been a member of the U.S. Army Air Corps during World War II, he was never an advocate of military force. Both "A Private Little War" and "The Omega Glory" spoke out against Federation involvement in planetary civil disputes—again, a risky position to take when the country was in the midst of the Vietnam War.

While he promoted liberal thinking like peace and harmony, Roddenberry wasn't afraid to take on the counterculture by pointing out that drugs and a simple, carefree life were not the answer to society's

(Above) The infamous interracial kiss scene

(Right) Kirk teaches the Hill People to fire guns in the Vietnam parable, "A Private Little War"

ills. This was the case in both "The Way to Eden" and "This Side of Paradise."

In "This Side of Paradise," Captain Kirk rejected the simple, loving, commune-like lifestyle of the colonists. For Kirk, the passive existence that was caused by alien spores—a drug of sorts—went against human nature. "Maybe we don't belong in Paradise," Kirk says. "Maybe we can't stroll to the music of lutes, Bones—we must march to the sound of drums."

Once again, STAR TREK was ahead of its time in pointing out the dangers of racism and intolerance as well as the dangers of drugs and surrendering one's individuality to a group consciousness.

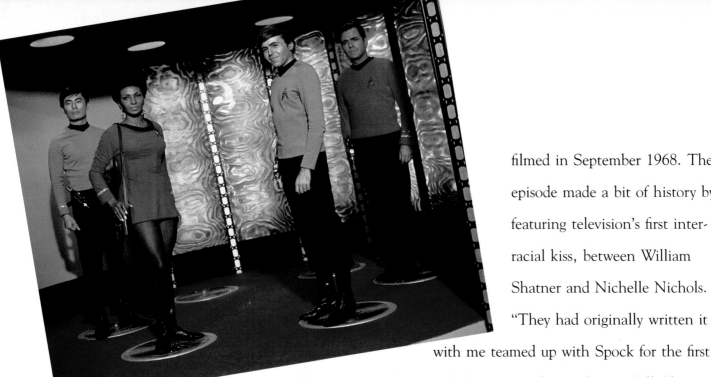

Cheerful and efficient transportees Mr. Sulu, Lieutenant Uhura, Mr. Chekov, and Mr. Scott

filmed in September 1968. The episode made a bit of history by featuring television's first interracial kiss, between William Shatner and Nichelle Nichols. "They had originally written it with me teamed up with Spock for the first interracial kiss," remembers Nichols. "My understanding is Bill Shatner took one look at the scene and said, 'No you will not! If anyone's going to be part of the first interracial kiss in television history, it's going to be me!' So they rewrote it."

The scene made the network executives extremely nervous; fearing that Southern affiliates might refuse to broadcast the episode, they asked the actors to shoot the scene two ways: one in which the kiss actually occurred, one in which it didn't. Nichols quips, "So because Bill and I are such staunch perfectionists and respect our craft and our profession, we did not balk at thirty-six takes!"

According to her, the only fan mail that protested came from "one guy who said, 'I'm a white Southerner, I believe in the separation of the races, but any time that a red-blooded American boy like Captain Kirk gets a beautiful gal like Lieutenant Uhura into his arms, he ain't going to fight it.' That was the big, major protest."

Unfortunately, STAR TREK could not survive its difficult Friday-night time slot. In February 1969, NBC announced that the show would be canceled. Ironically, "Turnabout Intruder," the final episode, was aired less

than six weeks before humans first set foot on the moon.

William Shatner reports that he felt great sadness, and a sense of anxiety about the future. For him, he says, "STAR TREK went out not with a bang but with a whimper, a cold sweat, and a stomach ache."

"We knew it was the graveyard slot," said DeForest Kelley. "We knew it was on its way out. We felt all along that we were doing something rather special, that this was a show that should not go off the air."

"I had mixed emotions," said Leonard Nimoy. "I felt tired and drained. It had become a battle to maintain the quality of the show. . . . You hate to see anything good die, but on the other hand, you hate to see anything good piddle its way into mediocrity or worse."

But STAR TREK was far from dead . . . as the fans soon proved.

The *Enterprise* crew near the end of their three-year television voyage

Part Two

STAR TREK®

THE IN-BETWEEN YEARS

Not long after STAR TREK was canceled, Paramount decided to syndicate the series. Now the show was no longer limited only to NBC affiliates; it could be shopped to countless stations, slipped into any time slot. As a result, independent stations quickly picked it up.

And something very interesting happened: STAR TREK became an enormous hit. Not only were its fans determined not to let the series die—they were going to make sure it lived long, and prospered. Gene Roddenberry and Majel Barrett discovered that their new mail-order business, Lincoln Enterprises, could barely keep up with the overwhelming demand for STAR TREK memorabilia. Indeed, Roddenberry stated at the time, "If I were getting six or eight letters a week about STAR TREK, I'd feel proud and successful. But I get a hundred letters a week addressed to me

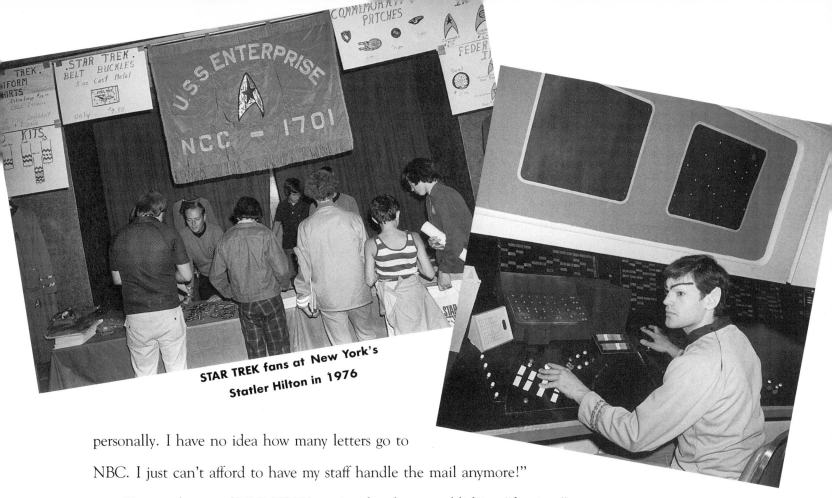

STAR TREK fans at New York's Statler Hilton in 1976

personally. I have no idea how many letters go to NBC. I just can't afford to have my staff handle the mail anymore!"

Hungry for new STAR TREK stories, fans began publishing "fanzines" and communicating with each other via newsletters. As their numbers grew, they began to gather. Soon STAR TREK clubs began to form; one of the most well known was the "Committee," which included as members Joan Winston, Devra Langsam, and Allan Asherman.

On the weekend of January 21–23, 1972, the first "national" STAR TREK Committee Convention was held in New York City. Five hundred fans were expected; well over three thousand packed inside the Statler-Hilton to listen to guest of honor Gene Roddenberry.

The convention featured other speakers (among them science-fiction greats Isaac Asimov and Hal Clement), as well as a dealers' room filled with fanzines, home-sewn "Star Trek" uniforms, phasers, tribbles, publicity photos, and "I Grok Spock" buttons. NASA provided a display of a one-third-size Apollo spacecraft and lunar module, plus a full-size authentic

STAR TREK fan Jonathan Harris (in Vulcan makeup) at Spock's science station in a mock-up of the bridge. Harris now makes a living as a STAR TREK convention promoter, running Dreamwerks Production Group, based in Boca Raton, Florida. The bridge mock-up was built by a young fan named Doug Drexler, who is now on the STAR TREK: DEEP SPACE NINE art department staff.

The Conventions as Asimov Sees Them
An Essay by Isaac Asimov

In 1972, a STAR TREK convention was held in New York. I was asked to attend, and I did.

In 1973, a second convention was held in New York. I was asked to attend, and I did.

In 1974, a third convention was held in New York. I was asked to attend, and I did.

In 1975, two conventions were held in New York, and I attended both. In 1976 . . . ditto.

For some reason this seems to strike many people (whether friends or strangers) as odd, and even humorous. At least, they begin to chuckle.

It is clear that their vision of such a convention is that it is attended by hordes of screaming subteen girls, all jumping up and down.

Well, there are subteen girls at these conventions, but they are not screaming and they are not jumping up and down. They are also not the only ones present. There are, in addition, subteen boys, teenage girls, teenage boys, grown women, and grown men.

And there are more of them, generally, than the sponsors of the convention expected—at least for the first two. At the first convention there were plans for 250 and 2,500 arrived. At the second convention, determined not to be caught napping, the sponsors planned for 4,000 and 7,000 arrived.

At the third convention there were 14,000, and in 1975, attendance was over 7,000 at each of the two conventions held only a month apart.

Was it chaos? It most certainly was not. There was the natural discomfort that came of trying to handle many more people than you had come prepared to handle, but I have never witnessed (in a reasonably long lifetime of attending conventions of all sorts: science-fiction, science, and business) any group of people as reasonable, as orderly, and as good-humored as at each of these conventions.

At the second convention, particularly, I remember the costume party with a large room filled out to the blue horizon with crowds of eager Trekkies, all watching the contestants with the most perfect decorum.

I remember the attendance at the talks, at my talks, for instance. I spoke to as many as 3,000 people, I estimate, with standing room only, in the back, and attention was total. When the talk was done and it was question time, a number of people lined up behind two microphones to take their turn at questioning while the rest of the audience remained fixed and orderly.

Friends Isaac Asimov and Gene Roddenberry in a happy moment

Then afterward, when there was an autograph session, there was a long line formed, and people waited patiently for half an hour and more to get to me.

These were the Trekkies, these were the supposedly screaming, jumping-up-and-down twelve-year-olds. Not so at all. These were enthusiastic people of all ages who had taken part in the STAR TREK experience, who had been and were participants in the most sophisticated example of science fiction on the television screen, and a little of whose lives had been permanently marked as a result.

The Trekkies are intelligent, interested, involved people with whom it is a pleasure to be, in any numbers. Why else would they have been involved in STAR TREK, an intelligent, interested, and involved show?

Only once, in fact, did the general order and decorum break at one of those conventions, and that was when Mr. Spock (well, Leonard Nimoy) made a brief appearance. And then the young women did do a little screaming—but you have to allow for hormones, after all.

space suit. And then there was the costume contest, which included a Klingon ambassador, a Vulcan warrior queen, and a Starfleet cadet in formal dress. . . .

Why did they do it? One of the convention organizers, Joan Winston, wryly notes that the motive certainly wasn't profit; her take of the proceeds came to the magnificent sum of $92.46. Organizers and attendees alike were there for one reason: because they loved STAR TREK. And all were excited by the pervasive rumor that Paramount was thinking about making the show again.

When asked at the convention whether STAR TREK might return, a dazed Gene Roddenberry replied, "I didn't think it was possible six months ago, but after seeing the enthusiasm here I'm beginning to change my mind. . . ."

He went on to explain STAR TREK's appeal: "The world is violent and unhappy, and it's ridiculous to have it as it is. That's what youth has been saying for the past dozen years, and that's what STAR TREK stood for. Youth is looking today at things like the violence in Northern Ireland and saying, 'My God! How is such a thing possible in the twentieth century?' So they dig a show that says we're not only going to have to love each other as Catholics and Jews, blacks and whites, but that if we go into space we're going to have to learn to relate to things that may look like giant slugs."

NBC was beginning to change its mind about STAR TREK's return, too. Partly because of the show's growing popularity in syndication and the visibility of fan conventions, the network decided to resurrect the series in its original guise. Their decision may have been at least in part due to the fact

Twenty-two-month-old Amanda Kendrick of Easton, Pa., has an alien encounter at the 1976 STAR TREK convention

Grace Lee Whitney and fans enjoy each other's company at the same 1976 convention

that NBC had recently switched to a new ratings system, based on demographics. (After the series was canceled, to its chagrin, NBC learned from a demographics expert that STAR TREK appealed to exactly the type of consumer the network was trying to reach, and was actually one of its most successful shows.) Network executives approached Roddenberry. But it was determined that the venture would be too expensive—Paramount said that rebuilding sets and replacing props and costumes would cost $750,000—so the project was dropped.

Yet it was again revived, this time in animated form, by Filmation, which granted Roddenberry creative control. Roddenberry became executive consultant, and Dorothy Fontana was brought in to function as producer, although the credits list her as "Associate Producer."

At first, for budgetary reasons, only William Shatner, Leonard Nimoy, DeForest Kelley, James Doohan, and Majel Barrett were brought in to provide the voices; but when Nimoy learned that George Takei and Nichelle Nichols had been left out, he protested. Takei recalls, "We owe a great deal

An animated Spock gazes into his viewer while his animated captain looks on

to Leonard for his integrity and his courage. He said, 'I will not be a party to this if two of the minorities who contributed to making STAR TREK what it was when we were on television cannot be incorporated.' . . . And it was because of that stand that Leonard Nimoy took that Nichelle and I were brought in on the animated series." Unfortunately, the budget simply didn't exist to bring in Walter Koenig to provide Chekov's voice, but Koenig

Kirk finds himself in a magical universe where technology fails to function in "The Magicks of Megas-tu"

provided input by writing the episode "The Infinite Vulcan." Many of the cast read for more than their original roles; James Doohan, who read the part of Scotty, often supplied several other voices. In the episode "Yesteryear," for example, he provided the voices of the Andorian, the Healer, and the Guardian of Forever.

Fontana solicited several writers from The Original Series to provide scripts for the animated show, and not a one turned her down. Samuel A. Peeples, Stephen Kandel, David Gerrold, Margaret Armen, and others (including Fontana herself with "Yesteryear") contributed episodes. Actor DeForest Kelley commented, ". . . most of the scripts were not written for children. They are adult scripts and some of them are very good, and would have made good [live-action] STAR TREK's."

Reviewers concurred. The *Los Angeles Times* said:

NBC's new animated STAR TREK is as out of place in the Saturday morning kiddie ghetto as a Mercedes in a soapbox derby.

Don't be put off by the fact it's now a cartoon. . . . It is fascinating fare, written, produced and executed with all the imaginative skill, the intellectual flare and the literary level that made Gene Roddenberry's famous old science fiction epic the most avidly followed program in TV history, particularly in high IQ circles.

NBC might do well to consider moving it into prime time at mid-season . . .

Certainly one of the finest episodes of the animated show was "Yesteryear," the only one written by Dorothy Fontana; her production responsibilities allowed no time for writing. She recalls, "It took three months to complete one episode from start to finish, and that's rushing. This was due to all of the handwork involved—the hand painting. The only thing that they could do fast was when you had duplicate cells, they could Xerox them. And they didn't have color Xeroxes then, so they all had to be hand painted."

Yesteryear

While Dorothy Fontana, original series story editor, served as associate producer of the animated STAR TREK series, she once again turned her considerable talents toward writing about Spock and his home planet, Vulcan, creating what became the show's finest and most popular episode, "Yesteryear."

Unfortunately, it was the only episode Fontana wrote for the show, since her role as producer allowed her no more time for writing. She recalled, "When I came to the [animated] show, I wanted to do at least one script." She knew she wanted to write for Spock, since he had always been her favorite character and the focus of her favorites of the episodes she had written, like "This Side of Paradise" and "Journey to Babel." And she kept thinking about the Guardian of Forever from Harlan Ellison's "The City on the Edge of Forever." "I thought, 'Gee, I could use that as a device and explore Spock some more. How had that relationship [between Spock and his father, Sarek] been before, why did it evolve?"

In "Yesteryear," Kirk, Spock, and Federation historians use the Guardian to explore the planet Orion's past. However, when they return to the *Enterprise,* no one recognizes Mr. Spock. When ship's records show that the child Spock was killed at age seven, the adult Spock realizes he must return to the past to save himself.

"Yesteryear" provided the most in-depth look at the planet Vulcan of any STAR TREK episode, with exotic scenery that would have been too expensive for *The Original Series'* budget. As Fontana explained, "That's the one thing I always loved about the animated show, that we could have any kind of alien or any kind of set. . . . It opened up a lot of worlds so that we could really show people strange new worlds and civilizations." Viewers meet the pet *sehlat* referred to in Fontana's episode "Journey to Babel," and learned about the *kahs-wan,* a Vulcan coming-of-age ritual.

In the episode, the child Spock is saved—but not without cost. His pet *sehlat,* I-Chaya, is mortally wounded attempting to protect him, and is euthanized. Network executives wanted the ending changed so that the animal did not die; they feared it would be too upsetting for younger viewers. But, Fontana noted, "Gene [Roddenberry] said, 'Trust Dorothy, she'll handle it.' I really appreciated his confidence in me. So I handled it, I think, in a sensitive way. We never had a single complaint."

With the Guardian of Forever in the background, McCoy checks out the time-traveling Spock in "Yesteryear"

Yet despite the amount of work, Fontana had great enthusiasm for the show's creative possibilities. "One thing I always loved about the animation was the simple fact that we could have *any* kind of aliens and *any* kind of environment, because you just draw them, and you don't have to worry about whether the seams show in the costume, or the makeup, or anything. . . .

"[With 'Yesteryear'] it was great; remember, up to that point, we'd never seen a Vulcan city of any kind. I could describe the way it should be laid out, to my mind, and they drew it. And you finally get to *see* a *sehlat*, which could only be referred to in 'Journey to Babel'. . . . You could do all sorts of wonderful things, in terms of aliens and settings and critters."

Indeed, the animated format allowed some interesting new additions to the *Enterprise* crew, including communications officer Lieutenant M'Ress, a "felinoid" with a long tail and purring voice. (Majel Barrett, who supplied M'Ress's voice, notes that she had to learn how to purr and talk at the same time.) Also added was three-armed, three-legged Lieutenant Arex.

The animated series (which coincidentally premiered September 8, 1973, seven years to the day after the original show first aired) lasted only twenty-two episodes before cancellation. It received a fitting send-off, winning the Emmy Award as the Best Children's Series for the 1974–75 season. (It was following in good company; the original STAR TREK and its actors had been nominated for Emmys for all three seasons.) Was STAR TREK finally destined to fade from the screen and its fans' memories?

Hardly. Paramount's talk of resurrecting the show on television arose again. The adventure was just beginning. . . .

Part Three

STAR TREK®

THE FILMS

I t all started when Paramount acquired the STAR TREK copyright from Desilu in the late 1960s, and decided to present the "property" as a syndication package. There were plenty of takers; in fact, the show became a hands-down hit in syndication.

By 1975, Roddenberry and Paramount were having serious talks about STAR TREK II. But the project soon evolved from TV series to a modest-budget $3 million movie.

Roddenberry immediately set to work on a first draft of the screenplay, and soon turned in "The God Thing," a story about a computer with damaged programming and delusions of godhood. It also contained some elements that readers will recognize: a transporter accident that scrambles bodies, and a scene that shows Spock as a postulant with the Vulcan Masters.

Paramount rejected Roddenberry's effort, but was determined to come up with a suitable script. Soon, a steady stream of writers were making their way onto—and off—the Paramount lot. In February 1976, writer Harlan Ellison jokingly told interviewer Tom Snyder, "There have been nine hundred and sixty-seven writers called in on this project. Last word, there was no script. They've got a director, they've got a start date. No script. I think they're going to stand there and whistle. Who knows?"

Finally, the writing team of Chris Bryant and Alan Scott came up with a story idea that Paramount liked, which involved the ancient Titans (who turn out to be our friends aboard the *Enterprise,* thanks to the magic of time

Mr. Spock tries to contact V'Ger in STAR TREK: THE MOTION PICTURE

63

Lieutenant Xon ''Star Trek II's Lost Vulcan''

As STAR TREK II entered preproduction, all *The Original Series'* actors were signed to reprise their roles, except for Leonard Nimoy. Needing a Spock replacement to fill a similar slot in the new stories to be told, Roddenberry developed Lieutenant Xon (Pronounced ''Zahn'') as the *Enterprise*'s Vulcan science officer. Intriguingly, Xon is clearly a character in the best tradition of some of STAR TREK's most popular characters: Spock, Data, and Odo.

The Writer's/Director's Guide for STAR TREK II begins its character description of Xon by asking, ''Can a twenty-two-year-old Vulcan on his first space voyage fill the shoes of the legendary Mr. Spock?'' This constant comparison of Xon with Spock was to be part of Xon's ongoing struggle to fit into the predominantly human environment of the *Enterprise*.

And, like the android Data, he would encounter many of the same frustrations and challenges. As the Guide goes on to say, ''Xon will be engaged in a constant struggle within himself to release his buried emotions to be more human-like for the sake of doing a good job . . . we'll get humor out of Xon trying to simulate laughter, anger, fear, and other human feelings.''

When the STAR TREK II television series became STAR TREK: THE MOTION PICTURE, Nimoy was finally signed to reprise his role as Spock. David Gautreaux, the actor who was cast as Xon, eventually appeared in the film as Commander Branch of the Epsilon 9 communications station destroyed by V'Ger.

The Vulcan that never was: David Gautreaux in full Vulcan regalia as Xon

Lieutenant Ilia ''My celibacy oath is on record''

*B*ecause she was a completely new character, and not a replacement, the Deltan navigator, Lieutenant Ilia, survived the transition from STAR TREK II, the series, to STAR TREK: THE MOTION PICTURE. The main difference in her role in the television script and the film version was that for television, since she was to be a regular character, she was restored to life by V'Ger at the end of the episode.

Like Xon's similiarity to other STAR TREK characters, Ilia shares a certain similarity to *The Next Generation*'s Deanna Troi—specifically, Troi's limited sensing ability. In the STAR TREK II Writer's Guide, Ilia is described as having ''the esper abilities common on her planet . . . the ability to sense images in other minds. Never words or emotions, only images . . . shapes, sizes, textures.''

However, Ilia's most notable characteristic was almost the complete opposite of Xon's. Where Xon had to struggle to overcome his repressed emotions,

Ilia had to struggle to keep one specific kind of emotion repressed. As the Guide explains, ''On 114-Delta V, almost everything in life is sex-oriented . . . it is simply the normal way to relate with others there. Since constant sex is not the pattern of humans and others aboard this starship, Ilia has totally repressed this emotion drive and social pattern.''

Again echoing *The Next Generation*, Ilia and Commander Will Decker, Kirk's second-in-command, share a relationship similar to that of Deanna Troi and Will Riker. Both couples had a romance in the past, which they try to put behind them now that they serve on the same starship.

Though Persis Khambatta auditioned for the role of Ilia in a bald cap, as did all the other actors trying for the part, when actual production on STAR TREK: THE MOTION PICTURE began, she did shave her scalp completely.

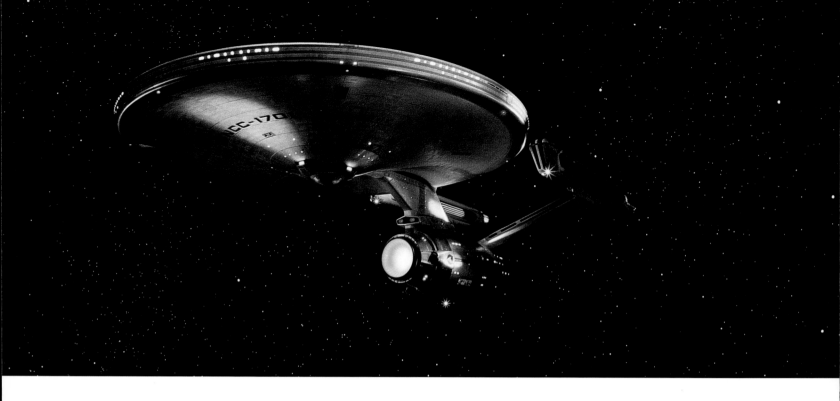

**The refitted *U.S.S. Enterprise*
NCC-1701**

had come so close to being resurrected as a television series, then a low-budget movie, then a series once more, was finally destined to become a major motion picture.

On March 28, 1978, Paramount held a press conference to announce that STAR TREK would soon become a $10 million movie. All the original cast, including Leonard Nimoy, had been signed and were in attendance that day. When asked whether he would find it difficult to play Captain Kirk after nine years away from the role, actor William Shatner replied, "I think Spencer Tracy said it best—'You take a deep breath and say the words.' Of course you have to have some years of experience to know how to say the words and suck in your breath. An actor brings to a role not only the concept of the character but his own basic personality, things that he is, and both Leonard and myself have changed over the years, to a degree at any rate, and we will bring that degree of change inadvertently to the role we re-create."

Leonard Nimoy had signed his contract barely twenty-four hours before, and at the time of the press conference, his character had yet to be written into the script. When asked why he had been so reluctant to play Spock once more, he stated, "It's really not a matter of reluctance. We had a lot of details to iron out. There have been periods of time when the STAR TREK concept was moving forward and I was not available. . . . When the project turned around and I was available again we started talking immediately. It has been complicated, it has been time-consuming. But there was never a question of reluctance to be involved in STAR TREK on my part. I've always felt totally comfortable about being identified with STAR TREK and being identified with the Spock character. It has exploded my life in a very positive way."

Veteran director Robert Wise (*West Side Story, The Sound of Music, The Day the Earth Stood Still*) was also present at the press conference, and said, "Science fiction is something that's always interested and intrigued me, but I've never had a chance to do this kind of show. I think it can make an absolutely fascinating picture. I'm looking forward to my involvement with all the cast and the marvelous special photographic effects that we can bring to it. I'm very excited."

But although the actors and directors had been signed, no script yet existed. It was finally chosen from the scrapped STAR TREK II series' pilot, "In Thy Image." Harold Livingston wrote the teleplay based on Alan Dean Foster's treatment; the teleplay was soon expanded by Livingston (with help from Roddenberry) into a screenplay.

Paramount spent an enormous sum on the film's special effects, first hiring Robert Abel and Associates, then Douglas Trumbull. The cost (which

Directed by Robert Wise

When Gene Roddenberry was contemplating which director would be right to direct the first "Star Trek" motion picture, writer Jon Povill, assistant to the producer, sent him a list of seven possibilities who would be good for the project:

1. Francis Ford Coppola
2. Steven Spielberg
3. George Lucas
4. Robert Wise
5. William Friedkin
6. George Roy Hill
7. Norman Jewison

Of course, Povill's memo went on to lament, such successful directors were no doubt busy with other projects and unavailable.

Wise was—at that moment. But by the time the original "Star Trek" cast had been reassembled and STAR TREK: THE MOTION PICTURE had been given the green light by Paramount, Wise was available and consented to direct the film.

Wise began his career as a film editor—it was he who edited the classic *Citizen Kane*—but soon moved into directing. His stellar track record includes *The Day the Earth Stood Still, The Haunting, The Sand Pebbles,* and *The Andromeda Strain.* He also directed *West Side Story* and *The Sound of Music,* both of which won Academy Awards for best director *and* best film.

Despite his reputation as a perfectionist, Wise was known for his incredible patience; after an unsuccessful "take," his harshest words were, "That's fine, let's try one more." In fact, a pool was soon organized on the ST:TMP set, with bets placed on the date of the first time Wise lost his temper. He never did. After filming wrapped, the pool organizers returned everyone's money.

Said Wise, in a preproduction interview: "One of the strengths of STAR TREK, in the TV series, has been the development of those characters and the strong impact that they had on the audiences. What I have to watch for on all of this is to see these characters that have been so well established are kept up in the foreground, are strong and vital and that we're involved with them, not just with the sight of these special effects."

Robert Wise on the set of STAR TREK: THE MOTION PICTURE

had gone from three to eight to ten million dollars) soon soared to $44 million—the most money, at that time, that Paramount had ever invested in a single film.

Yet for all its cost, STAR TREK: THE MOTION PICTURE was not warmly received by critics—in part because of its endless special effects, which it focused on at the characters' expense. Said Leonard Nimoy, "[Those in charge] had a concept. I think the concept was a kind of *2001* approach. Very cool. Very scientific. Steely gray. A very metallic film. That's what they wanted and, I suppose, they had the right to do it."

But despite STAR TREK: THE MOTION PICTURE's uneven reviews, the movie turned out to be a financial success; fans lined up for city blocks to see it. A pleased Paramount began making plans for a sequel.

In May 1980, Gene Roddenberry once again offered a movie treatment. This one dealt with the Klingons, who used the Guardian of Forever to go back and alter Earth history at the time of John F. Kennedy's assassination.

It Was the Best of Times: A bespectacled Kirk receives a quizzical glance from Lieutenant Saavik (Kirstie Alley) in STAR TREK II: THE WRATH OF KHAN

The U.S.S. Enterprise approaches space station Regula I

Paramount rejected that effort as well—right about the same time that they signed a gentleman by the name of Harve Bennett to a development deal. Bennett had served as a producer for CBS Television, then as vice-president of programming for ABC; he went on to become producer of "The Mod Squad" and executive producer of "The Six Million Dollar Man" and "The Bionic Woman."

Bennett remembers, "A week after I arrived there, they called me in to see Messrs. Bluhdorn and Diller and Eisner and Katzenberg, and to a lesser extent, the man who had brought me there, Gary Nardino, who was Head of Television at Paramount.

"It was a total surprise to me. Rather quickly, Bluhdorn got right to it and said, 'Can you make a STAR TREK II for a television-type budget? For less than forty-five million dollars?' I said, 'Where I come from, I could make four or five movies for that.' Which was prophetic."

Bennett said the following of his role in STAR TREK: "Credit for the success of the show, of course, goes to Gene Roddenberry. There's no disputing his genius. But it also goes to Gene Coon, the hardheaded rewriter who made a lot of things work.

"I think of myself, sometimes, as the Gene Coon of the feature movies. Fandom never understood the contribution made, notwithstanding Roddenberry's genius."

Bennett had never before watched an episode of the original STAR TREK; he immediately sat down and watched all seventy-nine episodes. His homework paid off; he became intrigued by the character of Khan Noonian Singh in "Space Seed," and soon came up with a story that dealt with Khan's

"Remember"

Scott and McCoy struggle to hold Kirk back from trying to save his dying friend

Our heroes land a Klingon Bird-of-Prey on the planet Vulcan

play to in STAR TREK. You have to play up those elements that are universal to human beings."

This time, the movie focused more on action, adventure, and the deep-felt camaraderie that had first made STAR TREK so popular. Critic Janet Maslin of *The New York Times* summed up its reception best: "STAR TREK II—Now that's more like it." *The Hollywood Reporter* called the film "far superior to its predecessor."

Once again, Paramount had another hit on its hands—and once again was eager to make a sequel. But would the movie have to be made without one of STAR TREK's most popular characters?

Maybe not. By the time Spock's death scene was filmed, Leonard Nimoy was beginning to have second thoughts. "I wasn't excited about not

Enter Harve Bennett

A multiple-choice question: What is the *Kobayashi Maru?*

    A. A third-class neutronic fuel carrier, carrying a crew of 81 and 300 passengers, last heard from in the vicinity of Sector Ten.

    B. The toughest test that cadets face in their years at Starfleet Academy.

    C. The brilliant solution to a very difficult public-relations problem.

    D. All of the above.

When Harve Bennett, executive producer of STAR TREK II: THE WRATH OF KHAN, asked Jack Sowards, author of the film's screenplay and cowriter of the story along with Bennett, to come up with a simulator test that had no solution, he had more than a great opening scene in mind.

"What I had designed," says Bennett, "was that the picture would open—and the audience would think we're in space, we're in a desperate situation, and it's very realistic, and all of a sudden, when they think the ship's going to blow up, a screen rises and James T. Kirk walks through the smoke and says, 'Well, you screwed that up.'"

Bennett smiles at the recollection. "If you think it was just sheer genius that I should decide to start a movie that way, it wasn't. I'm a pragmatist, a responsive player. What preceded the scene was the fact that word was out about my *first* idea for the film."

Bennett recalls that Leonard Nimoy had been reticent about reprising his role as Spock in the second STAR TREK motion picture. In early talks with Bennett, however, the actor had allowed that if the producer came up with a good story, he'd reconsider. And Bennett had done it. "I said, 'Leonard, you must be in this movie because we're going to kill you, and there'll be no more burden of putting the ears on.'"

Nimoy was intrigued. "He said, 'How will you kill me?' 'Just like Janet Leigh in the movie *Psycho,*' I told him. 'We're going to kill you one-third of the way into the movie, where they least expect it, and you're going to die heroically. And the rest of the movie will be, Let's get the bastards who killed Spock.' He said, 'I love it, it's wonderful, I'll sign.'"

But while the film was in preproduction, word leaked out about Spock's impending death, and all hell broke loose in fandom. "The world was screaming, 'You're going to kill Spock!' So I called Leonard and I said, 'Leonard, we're really screwed.

Admiral Bob, played by Harve Bennett in his cameo role from STAR TREK V: THE FINAL FRONTIER

We can't kill you now because everybody knows we're going to kill you like Janet Leigh.'"

However, Bennett soon realized that he might be able to use the public's knowledge to his advantage. "So I told Leonard, 'Okay, I promise, you're still going to die, but now you have to die at the *finish* of the movie.'" Nimoy agreed to the change, and Bennett set to work on "throwing tinfoil into the radar of those who knew," deliberately leaking rumors and half-truths about alternate endings being shot. The strategy worked; the filmmakers couldn't restore surprise, but they could establish ambiguity.

A similar technique was used in the film itself. Since the fans were expecting Spock to die in the beginning, á la *Psycho,* Bennett and Sowards fulfilled their expectations by killing Spock in the simulator during the first fifteen minutes of screen time. "It was a way of saying, 'Aha, just kidding, folks,' and knowing people would say, 'Oh, they weren't really going to kill him—they were just pulling our legs.' And then, when he died at the end, it caught them totally unawares!"

being Spock anymore," he says. "I was sad." But when he saw the finished film, he says, "I thought, 'That's very interesting. Where are they going with that?' The ending seemed to say something was going to happen."

And, of course, it *did* happen. But, Nimoy recalls, "It wasn't until they were getting ready to make TREK III that the studio called and asked if I wanted to be involved. I said I was very interested in being involved, to say the least. I wanted to direct the picture as well as act in it."

Harve Bennett soon set to work on the screenplay for STAR TREK III: THE SEARCH FOR SPOCK. He swears that he had in no way planned on bringing Spock back when he helped with *The Wrath of Khan*'s script. "I had to make a story out of the following givens," he remembers. "One, there is a casket on a planet that has been created by the re-formation of life forces, and life has been created from death. Two, 'There are always possibilities.' [Said in ST II by Captain Kirk as he leaves his dead friend behind on the Genesis planet.] Three, before he died Spock said, 'Remember.' . . . The puzzle was solved so easily that I think seventeen other people could have written the script to STAR TREK III."

Naturally, with a subtitle like *The Search for Spock,* could there ever be any doubt as to the Vulcan's return? As director Leonard Nimoy told *The New York Times,* "Well, look, we're calling the picture STAR TREK III: THE SEARCH FOR SPOCK. If we had Captain Kirk turn to the camera at the end of the picture and say, 'Sorry, we didn't find him,' people would throw rocks at the screen."

Christopher Lloyd as animal-lover Kruge, Kirk's nemesis in STAR TREK III: THE SEARCH FOR SPOCK

A disconsolate crew watches as the *Enterprise* sails to her fiery death

When Kirstie Alley demanded a substantial salary increase, she was replaced by Robin Curtis, who would go on to play Saavik in STAR TREK IV as well. STAR TREK III also included Mark Lenard's return in the role of Sarek, Spock's father. Other notable supporting actors included John Larroquette of "Night Court" fame, and Christopher Lloyd, both of whom played Klingons.

Since it was clear that the story's outcome could be safely predicted by fans, it was decided that the *Enterprise* would be destroyed in the film. Harve Bennett explains, "[STAR TREK III] needed something that would kind of rip you and startle you as a major surprise element. . . . We tried to keep it a secret. . . . Then, I'm sitting home watching television and the trailer [for the film] comes on and the narrator says, 'The last voyage of the *Starship Enterprise.*' Boom! And [the ship] blows up on my television set two weeks

Directed by Leonard Nimoy

Director Leonard Nimoy as his alter ego, Spock

When the producers of STAR TREK III: THE SEARCH FOR SPOCK called Leonard Nimoy to ask whether he would like to be involved with the project, Nimoy's immediate response was "You're damned right, I want to direct that picture!"

Nimoy's interest in directing was nothing new; as early as 1965, he audited the directors on "The Man from U.N.C.L.E.", which means that he was given access to the set and allowed to carefully observe the directors. In 1972, he directed an episode of "Night Gallery"; in 1982, an episode of "Powers of Matthew Star"; in 1983, an episode of "T. J. Hooker."

How did cast members react to having their former coworker directing them? According to William Shatner, "We were brothers in flesh and spirit. And now, suddenly, my brother was saying, 'You should do this,' and I would say, 'I think I should do that.' . . . It was more awkward in the beginning than any of the other films, but that slowly erased itself as I realized that Leonard had a point of view and knew what he was doing."

Fellow actor James Doohan reports, "[Nimoy] comes to the set with his homework done, the cinematographer's homework done, and if you allow him to, he would show you that he has your homework done, too. He's really terrific."

Nimoy the actor appeared only at the conclusion of STAR TREK III—and a good thing, too, he says, for he found self-direction extraordinarily challenging.

"The biggest problem I had, and this is really silly, but it happens that it was the scene in the sickbay of the Bird-of-Prey. Spock is unconscious and McCoy is talking to him. Now, not only am I in the scene, but I have to play the scene with my eyes closed. So I can't even look to see if the actor I am playing the scene with is looking anything like I think he should look. It drove De Kelley crazy. He swears that I was trying to direct him with the movement and flutter of my eyelids. It was very difficult. In a sense I was very pleased and relieved that the design of the story allowed me to do a minimal amount of performing."

Sizing himself up as a director, Nimoy allows, "I'm probably somewhere in between Bob Wise and Nicholas Meyer. Not as precise as Bob, not as imaginative or rough-edged as Nick. I think the major difference, and for me the most important difference, is my attitude toward the story and the actors. They [Wise and Meyer] are looking for a different kind of final product than I am."

STAR TREK III: THE SEARCH FOR SPOCK was a hit. Nimoy was subsequently offered the directorial reins for STAR TREK IV, which—to date—remains the most popular of the STAR TREK films. After its release, Nimoy became a much-sought-after director. He went on to direct the 1987 hit *Three Men and a Baby* as well as the critically acclaimed film *The Good Mother* (1988).

The cetacean probe approaches Earth in STAR TREK IV: THE VOYAGE HOME

But despite the lack of utter surprises, the picture was a rousing success. Reviewers were uniformly enthusiastic. According to the *Los Angeles Times,* "For all its spectacle in space, its humanity once again outweighs its hardware, and its innocence is downright endearing." Said *USA Today:*

Leonard Nimoy boasted years ago he could direct a better STAR TREK movie than the first two because he has a better sense of what made the TV series a hit. And he was right. STAR TREK III: THE SEARCH FOR SPOCK is the best *Star Trek* movie of the three, and the closest to the original spirit created by producer

Gene Roddenberry in the mid-nineteen-sixties . . .

Who knows? Considering how well Spock's spirit traveled after death, maybe the *Enterprise* will be rescued in STAR TREK IV. Surely there will be a IV, and we can hope Nimoy will again be at the controls.

The Streets of San Francisco: Spock and Kirk take on the twentieth century

And so he was, in STAR TREK IV: THE VOYAGE HOME, to date the most popular and financially successful of the films. The plot involved time travel and a certain pair of humpback whales named George and Gracie—but what filmgoers remember most about the movie was its sense of

exuberance and fun, the very quality that William Shatner spoke of when he
said, "There is a texture to the best STAR TREK hours that verges on
tongue-in-cheek but isn't . . . it's as though the characters within the play
have a great deal of joy about themselves, a joy of living . . . you play it with
the reality you would in a kitchen-sink drama written for today's life." Harve
Bennett called the quality "tap dancing," the ability to convey a sense of joie
de vivre even in the midst of a seriously dramatic moment.

Originally, a story was planned using Eddie Murphy as a twentieth-
century con man who manages to get involved with the *Enterprise* crew. But

Son of *Enterprise*: The new, improved *U.S.S. Enterprise* NCC-1701-A

Paramount was reluctant to combine its two biggest moneymakers into one movie, fearing it might reduce profits.

Says Leonard Nimoy, "The central aspect of what the movie was about, the plot, came out of a conversation that I was having with a scientist friend of mine. It was agreed, very early on, that we wanted to do a time-travel story going backward. A trip back from the twenty-third century, close to contemporary times. The reason for making this trip is out of a major concern about the things that we are losing from this planet today—intentionally, consciously, or otherwise."

Nimoy had the monumental task of both performing and directing, which he found a challenge. "It would be much easier if I were only doing one or the other. It was tough. I wouldn't recommend it."

The screenplay is credited to Steve Meerson and Peter Krikes (who wrote the original Eddie Murphy–centered script) *and* the team of Harve Bennett and Nicholas Meyer, which once again did a fast and furious rewrite. Bennett remembers, "I did an incredible amount of work in acts one and three. Nicholas did passionate and funny [things with] the middle part of it which set the tone. And we were racing along new channels, asking, 'Do you think it's going to be funny? Do you think people are going to laugh?' . . . I was influenced more by the irreverence of Nick Meyer on STAR TREK II, which had proven to me, against my kicking and screaming, that you could have fun with STAR TREK without losing its sting."

"Harve is a very fine constructionist," says Leonard Nimoy, "and Nick has the kind of humor and social comment, gadfly attitude that I very much wanted in this movie. I wanted it to be much lighter in tone and I wanted it to feel, in the writing of it and the shooting of it and in the performances, much more lighthearted."

He also saw to it that all of the STAR TREK characters—not just the "Big Three"—were involved. Walter Koenig, whose character Chekov stops passersby on San Francisco streets to inquire about where he might find "nuclear wessels," was pleased. "Chekov was a delight for me in STAR TREK IV," he reports. "He has been most successful when he has been put in comedic situations—but I feel I'm up to handling anything that's written for the character."

Back in the U.S.S.R.

On June 26, 1987, a STAR TREK film finally made it to the then-Soviet Union, when Leonard Nimoy and Harve Bennett introduced the film STAR TREK IV: THE VOYAGE HOME to a huge Moscow audience.

Nimoy explains: "The World Wildlife Fund made an arrangement with the Russian government to put a moratorium on commercial whale hunting. The World Wildlife Fund asked our permission to show STAR TREK IV in Moscow as part of the celebration of the moratorium." For Nimoy, the most thrilling aspect of the visit was the opportunity to visit the Ukrainian village from which his parents had emigrated. "I was very excited about it," he recalls. "I had just finished shooting *Three Men and a Baby*, literally, the night before I got on the plane to fly to Russia. I was physically drained when I got there, but I was carried along on the sheer excitement of being in Russia showing this movie in Moscow. Then, I went from Moscow into the Ukraine, by plane from Moscow to Lvov, and then a five-hour train ride across the Ukraine. It was a great thing. It was kind of a closure, because I've been hearing about that village all of my life—stories my parents and grandparents told me. And to be there firsthand and see it and understand what it is all about was a great thrill. The whole thing was the most emotionally and physically draining experience you can imagine."

Says Harve Bennett of the visit, "Running STAR TREK IV in Moscow was an extraordinary experience . . . the reactions, the laughs, the sighs came in exactly the same places as in Westwood [in the LA area]. The highlight was introducing the movie to an audience of the Russian equivalent of the Academy [of Motion Picture Arts and Sciences]—'Domkino'—House of Film. It was an audience of around eight or nine hundred . . . . I introduced it speaking through a translator.

"There were two noteworthy things about the translation. One was that the word *humpback*, in Russian, is *gorbach*. Actually, Gorbachev means *son of humpback*. It is a family name, and, of course, disassociated from its literal meaning. But the roots of the word are there. So my friend who was doing the Russian subtitles in the Cyrillic alphabet advised us of that, and said in his judgment that it could get a snicker of the wrong kind. Particularly since Scotty makes a little pun, 'Humpback people?' Just for safety's sake, we called the whales something else in Russian.

"The other thing, the one single most rewarding moment of my STAR TREK life, happened at the end of STAR TREK IV in Moscow on a line that was really kind of a character line, a 'slight smile' kind of line. They're on their way out to spacedock to pick up the 'gift' from a grateful Starfleet, which we find out in a minute is going to be *Enterprise*. But their skeptical speculation, mainly by Bones, is they'll get something less than they had. And Bones says the line, 'We'll get a freighter. The bureaucratic mentality is the only constant in the universe.' That line in Moscow got the biggest laugh I have ever heard! They roared, they stood up, they applauded. You couldn't hear the end of the picture. It was absolutely a messenger—a messenger of what was to come."

Uhura and Chekov aboard that "nuclear wessel," the *U.S.S. Enterprise*

Unfortunately, the scene in STAR TREK IV in which Sulu meets his great-great-grandfather was cut from the film; however, George Takei still has nothing but praise for Nimoy as a director.

Both Mark Lenard and Jane Wyatt returned in their roles as Sarek and Amanda, Spock's parents. Says Wyatt, "[Normally] I don't like acting with somebody who's also directing, because you're talking to them and in your close-up, he's looking to make sure the lights are all right, etc., and he's not concentrated. But I liked Leonard very much. He was an extremely good director and I thought the picture was good."

The film was a record-breaking box-office smash. As producer Ralph Winter notes, "It reached out to an audience beyond the STAR TREK fans. We deliberately wanted a movie that would be accessible to people who had never seen a STAR TREK film. And I think we accomplished that."

The critics agreed. *USA Today* said, ". . . the unequaled sequel will satisfy the most devout Trekkie and still delight those who don't know a Romulan from a Tribble. . . . This script turns Kirk and company into the most uproarious out-of-towners to hit the Bay Area since the Democrats in 1984. . . . Anyone who sees *Voyage Home* will be marking the calendar for the series' next stardate."

Three years later, in STAR TREK V: THE FINAL FRONTIER, William Shatner got his opportunity to direct and come up with the story line. Although Harve Bennett was burned out on STAR TREK and had already made the decision to move on, Shatner went to him and convinced him once again to produce. Bennett wanted to work with Nicholas Meyer again on the script, but when Meyer was not available, he brought in a young

The *Enterprise*-A is pursued by a Klingon Bird-of-Prey in orbit over the mystical planet Sha Ka Ree

writer, David Loughery (screenwriter for the films *Dreamscape* and *Flashback*).

Shatner immensely enjoyed his opportunity to direct. He says:

I had the most joyful experience of my life on *Star Trek V*. And it was also full of the major joys and major sorrows of anything I've ever done. I remember having the urge to direct some of the STAR TREK television episodes, but at the time, I felt directing was beyond my capabilities. I've been directing all my life in theater, and I did a number of television shows, like "T. J. Hooker." But this was totally different—no relationship to anything I've ever done before. An eye-opener and a life-changing, mind-altering experience. But I've learned a great deal. I've learned how to put a film together. I've learned how to deal with certain people. I've learned the art of compromise and I've learned the deadliness of compromise. And the necessity of perhaps compromising with compromise.

Once again, the STAR TREK cast members were directed by one of their own—and all had nothing but good to report. "Shatner is great as a director," reports Leonard Nimoy, "a lot of fun, very earnest and hardworking. He's a bright guy and very energetic and we have a good relationship, and I'm having a good time. He asks advice sometimes, but he doesn't ask how to shoot the picture—that's all his vision. We talk about dealing with studio personalities, internal politics of filmmaking."

According to DeForest Kelley, Shatner is "a delight to work for, and I was very impressed with his directorial ability."

"I know that Bill had a lot of pressures on him," says George Takei. "And I have enormous admiration for his ability to block that kind of pressure from seeping onto the set itself. I know there were budgetary pressures and schedule pressures that were intense on Bill. But he was very, very energetic, enthusiastic, supportive, and helped create a good creative atmosphere. I'm grateful to him for that."

The story line involved Spock's older half-brother, Sybok (portrayed by actor Laurence Luckinbill), and his quest to find "God," who turns out to be a powerfully evil entity. The story line was reminiscent of "The God Thing"

Directed by William Shatner

While the critics may have been stingy in their praise for William Shatner's motion-picture directorial debut, no one who worked with him on STAR TREK V: THE FINAL FRONTIER can deny that director William Shatner put all of his heart and soul—and sheer physical stamina—into it.

"A film has to move—it's called 'motion picture,' after all—you have to make it move," explains Shatner. "The characters as well as the camera have to be in motion. I wanted to push the characters in a slightly different direction, with tempo, vigor, animation, intention. Every scene was fashioned with that in mind, making the characters move."

The characters—or rather the actors who played them—noticed.

"I think that STAR TREK V is the most physical of the movies we've done," Leonard Nimoy observes. "I think that reflects Bill—Bill's energy, Bill's sense of what movies are for him, and what he always enjoyed doing during the series. I'm talking about sheer physical running and jumping."

"There are things that I had to do in the film that I hadn't done for a long time, that I haven't been called upon to do," adds DeForest Kelley. "Bill has great energy and my hope when I started STAR TREK V was that he could bring some of that energy into it. I was very pleased to see that he brought it along in fine style."

Shatner approached the extreme demands of working both sides of the camera the way a runner prepares for a marathon. "I got myself into the best shape I've been in for years, with aerobics, strength exercising, and stretching," he notes. And as with a runner, the adrenaline rush of the filmmaking process carried him beyond mere mortal frailties. "My body woke me up every day at around four or four-thirty A.M. no matter what time I got to sleep, and I'd lie in bed for an hour before I got up—dreaming, running the film through my mind, trying to hone a moment so that when I came to the set I knew exactly what the camera should be doing, what I should be doing, and what the actors should be doing."

Although Shatner was keen to keep his actors moving at the same pace he set for himself, he was always watchful of their safety. That was never more apparent than when he got them up on horseback in the middle of the Mojave Desert. "I got up on my horse the first night and Bill came over to give me instructions," recalls Nimoy. "Bill's a very serious horseman and he was worried about me, telling me, 'You press your knees and the horse does this, you pull the reins and the horse does that.'"

The extra attention amused Nimoy. "I don't think he knew that I'd started riding in Westerns thirty-seven years before. The first Western I did was with Rex Allen and Slim Pickens at Republic. I played a lot of Indians, riding all kinds of saddles and even riding bareback. But I didn't want to embarrass Bill by saying, 'I know—I'm okay on a horse.'"

STAR TREK V: THE FINAL FRONTIER:
Shatner directs his daughter
Melanie on the bridge set

Spock's long-lost
half-brother, Sybok
(Laurence Luckinbill)

and V'Ger in STAR TREK: THE MOTION PICTURE, and unfortunately,

**Spock jet-boots by to visit his
El Capitan–climbing captain**

was panned by reviewers. STAR TREK V's box-office take was the lowest of

the first five films. Executive producer Ralph Winter philosophized, "Hind-

sight is, of course, twenty-twenty. You look back on it and say, 'Well, gosh,

when you have a story that's going to find God, you necessarily have to show

that.' And that's always going to be disappointing. . . . There were similari-

ties, of course, with V'Ger. Maybe our mistake was not recognizing more of

that. . . ."

Despite *The Final Frontier*'s disappointing box-office take, Paramount

Scott reassures Kirk that he "knows the ship like the back of my hand"—seconds before his unfortunate encounter with a low-hanging pipe

was determined to celebrate STAR TREK's twenty-fifth anniversary with another movie. Harve Bennett signed on to write the script, and came up with STAR TREK VI: THE FIRST ADVENTURE, which dealt with young Kirk and Spock's adventures at Starfleet Academy. But Paramount was nervous about the thought of making a movie without Shatner and Nimoy, and so the story was rewritten to include flashback scenes featuring the adult Kirk and Spock. Even so, Roddenberry and the actors lobbied hard for at least one more reunion of the entire original cast.

Paramount finally rejected the Academy idea, and Bennett left, saying, "I've had two five-year missions. They were almost entirely successful. The last one dropped off, but I don't think it was a failure. I'd like to take my championship rings and go on to another arena."

Western Legends

During the filming of STAR TREK V: THE FINAL FRONTIER, critics began to suggest, for the first time, that perhaps the crew of the *Starship Enterprise* was growing a bit long in the tooth for their exploits in space. Even some members of the crew—one of whom had lived and died and lived again onscreen—seemed more cognizant of their own mortality, which may have prompted this recollection from Leonard Nimoy:

"In the early sixties, I was working on a job at MGM and it was a lunch break. I was walking down

The six-shooter-totin' trio in "Spectre of the Gun"

the main street there and I saw two guys, obviously doing a Western, dressed in cowboy outfits, walking side by side, keeping stride. As they got a little closer I began to hear their spurs, clink, clink, clink, coming down the street. When they got closer and I got a better look, I saw they were pretty well along in years—these were not kids—a couple of big old cowboys. And then I realized that it was Randolph Scott and Joel McCrea walking side by side. I got chills! They were working on Sam Peckinpah's picture *Ride the High Country*, a wonderful film that deals with a couple of old-time cowboys coming to the end of the line. And here they were, a couple of old-time cowboy actors coming to the end of *their* line.

"Now, every once in a while, when Bill and De and I are walking down the street on the lot, I'll see people looking at us and I get that image in my head. And I wonder if people think that about us—'Here they are, the old guys, walking down the street.'"

A Warm Glow: The Big Three in a relaxed moment by the campfire in STAR TREK V

A short time later, Paramount head Frank Mancuso called Leonard Nimoy and said that the studio would like to have one more STAR TREK movie in time for the twenty-fifth anniversary of STAR TREK in 1991. Leonard Nimoy very quickly came back to him with the idea of doing a film in which the Klingons were experiencing trouble that mirrored what was happening in the Soviet Union at the time. Nimoy postulated that the Klingons had suffered a Chernobyl-like disaster which was compounded by the fact that they had overextended themselves on military spending.

The *U.S.S. Enterprise* under attack from General Chang's cloaked Bird-of-Prey vessel

McCoy fights to save Klingon Chancellor Gorkon's life while a distraught Kirk and Chang look on

Mancuso asked if the story would include a character similar to Gorbachev and Nimoy replied, "Absolutely." Nimoy agreed to be the executive producer of the film and indicated that he would like Nicholas Meyer to write and perhaps direct the movie. In the event that Meyer decided not to direct, Nimoy would direct it himself or find someone else for the job.

Nimoy met with Nicholas Meyer in what Nimoy describes as a "classic walk on the beach meeting." The two men discussed the idea for the film, and decided that Kirk would be the "point man" of the peace effort—the logic being that just as only a conservative like Nixon could go to China, only a man with Kirk's history of antagonism toward the Klingons could

Directed by Nicholas Meyer

Nick Meyer is not just a director, but a writer of renown whose novels include *The Seven Per Cent Solution, The West End Horror,* and *Black Orchid.* He also penned the screenplay *Time After Time* (based on Karl Alexander's novel *The Time Travelers*) and went on to direct the popular film. Meyer also adapted his own book *The Seven Per Cent Solution* into a script, for which he received a 1978 Oscar nomination; he has also received two Emmy nominations—one for cowriting *The Night That Panicked America,* and one for directing the television movie *The Day After.*

Interestingly, before he was asked to direct STAR TREK II: THE WRATH OF KHAN, Meyer had never seen an episode of STAR TREK. However, he didn't view that as a hurdle. "There are only two kinds of art," he said, ". . . good and bad. The only allegiance to the content of STAR TREK that I felt I owed was to that which struck me as good. I felt that I owed *no* allegiance to anything that was bad, for any reason whatever. My feeling, when I was working on [STAR TREK II] was to divide things up with that in mind. I didn't like the costumes from any other version, so I made new costumes. I didn't like the sets, so we reworked the sets. If I didn't like the dialogue, I reworked the dialogue."

In approaching STAR TREK II, Meyer decided that he wanted to give the film an "adventure on the high seas" feel:

"I said I'd really like to stretch the nautical analogy. I said it should be like Captain Horatio Hornblower in outer space. I made everyone on the set watch the movie version of Hornblower. The young midshipman who gets killed . . . he's stolen right out of that movie. And it was interesting, because when I first spoke to Bill Shatner about my idea, he said, 'That's interesting; that was also Gene Roddenberry's original take on it.' So far, so good. But I really wanted to pursue it. I had ship's bells, and botswain's whistles and all that sort of stuff. And we very much stressed the idea of the ships as galleons in space . . . And the other thing I kept saying: Because I'm not very interested in science fiction but I *am* interested in stories about people, the only reason for me to make this movie is if they can be real. Why can't they do things that we do now? I hate when they say 'negative' when they mean 'no.' "

The "high seas" theme continued in STAR TREK VI: THE UNDISCOVERED COUNTRY, which Meyer wanted to have a claustrophobic, gripping *The Hunt*

Nick Meyer directing the action in STAR TREK VI

for Red October feel. (The phrase "the undiscovered country,") taken from *Hamlet,* refers to death. Meyer had originally used it as the subtitle for STAR TREK II; it was changed at the last minute by an executive. "And it just so happens," Meyer says, "that in slightly different context, the name is as applicable to STAR TREK VI as it was for STAR TREK II."

Meyer's films tend to include a generous sprinkling of literary allusions—from *A Tale of Two Cities* and Milton in STII, and Shakespeare in STVI. (He co-wrote the screenplay for STAR TREK IV and cowrote the screenplay for STAR TREK VI with Denny Martin Flinn, based on a story he cowrote with Leonard Nimoy and Flinn.) Says he, "I think I also make movies primarily for people who read. It doesn't mean that only people who read can get off on them, but the more you read the more you're going to get off on the little touches of that type that are in there."

Commenting on his career as a writer and director, Meyer mused, "I'm the most fortunate person I know. I realize it every day of my life. There's not a day that I don't walk onto a set and say, 'Oh my God, I can't believe I'm doing this!' "

succeed in winning peace between the Federation and the Klingon Empire. This idea became the touchstone for the film's dramatic tension.

In the end, Nimoy acted as executive producer of STAR TREK VI and Nicholas Meyer directed from a script he co-wrote with Denny Martin Flinn.

In the production, there was a sense, from the very beginning, that this would very likely prove the final film with all of the original cast. Said William Shatner of the experience of acting in STAR TREK VI, "It was a very pleasant experience filled with nostalgia even in the act of making it, realizing that this was the last and that I would probably not work with these

The accused listen to the Klingon translation of courtroom proceedings in STAR TREK VI: THE UNDISCOVERED COUNTRY

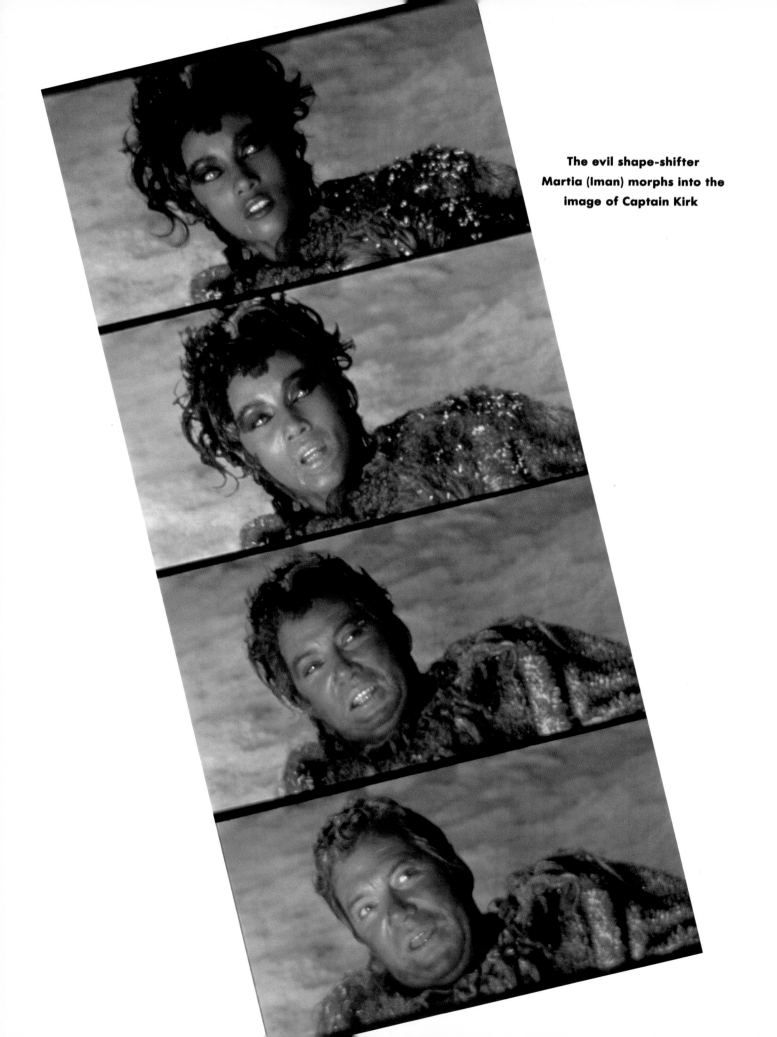

The evil shape-shifter Martia (Iman) morphs into the image of Captain Kirk

people again, especially Leonard Nimoy and DeForest Kelley, who are old friends."

"You've got to understand that making STAR TREK movies has always been like getting together for a family reunion," Leonard Nimoy adds. "When we got together this time, we all knew this was going to be the *last* family reunion. There was a lot of emotion attached to this one, because we knew we were never going to do this again."

"It's hard to believe," says De Kelley. "Sometimes you think, 'My God, has it really been twenty-five years? Who would have ever thought we would still be together for these many years?'"

The film was an action-packed story of political intrigue that featured actress Kim Cattrall in the role of Valeris, Spock's protégé-turned-traitor. Meyer gave the film a relentless pace and a gritty, claustrophobic feel. He says, "If I were designing spaceships for STAR TREK from scratch, I would probably have designed a much more claustrophobic world because it's much more dramatic."

The film was a hit with critics and fans alike. Buoyed by another financial success, Paramount was ready for the next sequel. But now it was time to pass the torch to a new generation of STAR TREK characters. . . .

Star Trek: Generations

If you should ask anyone who worked on the final season of STAR TREK: THE NEXT GENERATION to define "Hell," the response is likely to be "March 1994." That month was, without a doubt, the most frenzied period in the lives of dozens of talented people on the Paramount lot, thanks to the overlapping shooting schedules of the final episode of the series and the seventh STAR TREK motion picture, STAR TREK: GENERATIONS. As costume designer Robert Blackman, who found himself simultaneously working on the last episode and the movie—not to mention *Deep Space Nine* and the upcoming STAR TREK: VOYAGER—put it, "I don't have a life!"

And so it was for the actors, the writers, and the production staff. The *Next Generation* actors found themselves being fitted for movie costumes even as they memorized their lines for the next scene in "All Good Things . . .," a task made even more arduous by the fact that the complicated story line of that final episode required the actors to keep track of where their characters were in time on any given day of shooting. The cast would have only a few days to rest between the wrap of the series and their first appearances for the movie, which had already begun filming on a nearby soundstage.

"It was a chaotic, exhausting juncture," reports writer Brannon Braga, who teamed with Ronald D. Moore on both "All Good Things . . ." and *Generations.*

During those weeks of overlapping production, it was easy to feel a bit schizophrenic. Behind-the-scenes personnel would leave one soundstage, where a bewildered Captain Picard was "leaping" from the early days of his service on the *Enterprise*-D to a point in time after his retirement from Starfleet, and walk to another stage just a few yards away, where a now-retired Captain Kirk was unhappily attending the dedication ceremony for Starfleet's newest vessel, the *Enterprise*-B. "It was kind of like being in one of those 'parallel universe' episodes," laughs one crew member.

STAR TREK: GENERATIONS began filming on March 28, 1994, at Paramount, making use of a number of soundstages across the lot, including Stages 8 and 9, home for seven years to *The Next Generation*'s *Enterprise* D. Over the course of shooting the movie, off-the-lot locations took the crew from the high seas (off the coast of Marina del Rey) to the low desert (an ancient seabed called the Valley of Fire, which is near Las Vegas). The process of bringing *The Next Generation* to the big screen was not a routine matter, even for the people who have worked on the series for years. "When you sit down to watch *The Next Generation* on television, you have certain expectations," says writer Braga. "But when you go to a movie, you expect Big Screen Excitement, and that means bigger action, bigger humor, and bigger events. We were allowed to take more dramatic risks and show changes in characters' personalities that we never could have done within the series. We do some radical things with Data, for example, that could be quite controversial, that we couldn't do on a weekly show."

Some dramatic changes were deemed necessary for the look of the *U.S.S. Enterprise* 1701-D as well. "The difference between a thirty-feet-high, eighty-feet-wide movie screen and a twenty-inch diagonal video screen means that the level of detail must be increased," explains production designer Herman Zimmerman. "Film has a much higher resolution; the TV medium is much more forgiving. So we've increased the level of detail on all the basic sets that I originally designed for the series. We're using every set except the observation lounge, and we've added a couple of new sets." The most interesting one, according to Zimmerman, is Stellar Cartography. "It's a three-story set. You enter on the second-story level and in front of you is a three-hundred-degree graphic representation of our

Chekov, Kirk, and Scotty on the bridge of the *U.S.S. Enterprise* NCC-1701-B

Captain Picard in full 19th century sailing regalia

universe. Some very important story points are made in the changing graphics on that enormous circular screen," Zimmerman adds mysteriously.

There is less mystery to the changes the audience may—or may not—detect on the bridge. "We've added a platform under the captain, and added some command stations right and left of the horseshoe. And the colors are somewhat different." In *The Next Generation* television series, the ceiling above the bridge was a light-toned ocher, Zimmerman notes. "Gene Roddenberry wanted the bridge to feel very comfortable, very much like a pleasant, large hotel in space," he says. "That color served us very well on television, because you light things very flat. Of necessity, when you do a new show every seven days, you can't stop and light every scene and every camera angle for the romance of it, which you *must* do for a motion picture."

So the ceiling of the *Enterprise*'s bridge in *Generations* was changed to a metallic bronze. Predicts Zimmerman: "I'm expecting the audience to see it in the film and say, 'Oh, that's what it really looked like.' All we've done is take basically the same color tones and darken them several values, so the actors will stand out against the background more."

While *Generations* has as much in the way of action and special effects as any of its six predecessors, it also has, at its core, the profound sense of humanity that the films haven't really explored since STAR TREK II: THE WRATH OF KHAN. "This film is about family and mortality and growing old," says Braga. "It's the concern that all of us

have about death, about what it means to die if you have no family, the question of how, in essence, do you continue if you don't have family?"

The built-in emotional power of the movie comes, in part, from the audience's sensing "the baton being passed" from the crew of the original *Enterprise* to that of *The Next Generation*. STAR TREK VI: THE UNDISCOVERED COUNTRY subtly prepared the viewers for the bridging of that gap with a guest appearance by Michael Dorn as an ancestor of his *Next Generation* character Worf, the introduction of the first tentative steps toward a Federation peace pact with the Klingons, and, in a moving visual tribute, the "sign-off" of *The Original Series'* actors.

But the aptly named *Generations* will go further than that. "I think the whole movie is a symbolic passing of the baton," says writer Ronald D. Moore, "the christening of a new *Enterprise* to start the picture, then Kirk stepping aside, and then the biggest passing of the baton of all, the two captains coming together."

Generations will also include some of the best performances ever from some very familiar faces. Scenic art supervisor Michael Okuda, who has spent more than enough time on STAR TREK sets to dull the sense of wonder that most fans experience when they watch the series or the movies, reports that the film's initial scenes with *The Original Series* cast were exciting. "There is a real chemistry to the actors that shines in this picture," he notes enthusiastically. "I was on the set watching some interaction between them and suddenly it became one of those rare moments when they ceased to be 'William Shatner and Walter Koenig' and they were, literally, Kirk and Chekov. There was a magic there that I haven't felt since I first watched *The Original Series*."

The crew of the *U.S.S. Enterprise* 1701-D on a 19th century sailing vessel

Part Four

Photography by Gary Hutzel

STAR TREK depicted us in reckless youth, with a Starship captain who tamed space as vigorously as we laid claim to the future . . . STAR TREK: THE NEXT GENERATION reveals the child grown—a little more polished, but also more complacent. And if there's a bit of gray and a wrinkle or two, so much the better.

—Gary D. Christenson, TV Guide, July 23, 1988

I t began in 1986, when Paramount executives couldn't help noticing that they had a string of hit STAR TREK movies on their hands. If STAR TREK could successfully make the transition to film, why couldn't another television series do just as well? With, say, an all new cast, so that salaries wouldn't be prohibitively expensive, and so that the original actors could continue making movies without interruption. And if the new show caught on, well, then someday there could be movies with *that* cast, and then maybe . . .

Paramount soon offered Gene Roddenberry creative control of the project. It was decided that, unlike the aborted STAR TREK II, this series would not be a thinly disguised rehash of *The Original Series*, but a brand-new look at the STAR TREK universe some seventy-eight years in the

future. Instead of a "space Western" with shoot-outs between the bad guys and our heroes, the new show would favor a pacifistic, intellectual approach to solving problems. Nor would there again be the dominant triad of captain, doctor, Vulcan science officer; instead, the emphasis would be on a "family" of characters, giving the show a more "ensemble" feel. As Roddenberry said, "I don't think we need a retread crew with people playing the same kinds of roles. I'm not at all sure we'll have a retread Vulcan. I would hate to think our imagination is so slender that there aren't other possibilities to think about."

As fate—or luck—would have it, all four networks (including Fox) turned down the new STAR TREK, which actually suited Roddenberry, who

The U.S.S. Enterprise
NCC-1701-D

remembered his battles with NBC censors, just fine. Paramount made the decision to syndicate the new show, which meant that instead of being carried by individual television stations who were part the group of stations that made up a network, STAR TREK would be sold to individual stations in each market.

With a budget of over $1 million, Roddenberry went about the task of gathering his creative team. He immediately hired STAR TREK veteran Robert Justman, who recalls: "I wanted to work with Gene again. We worked very well together and we always had a good time. And I wanted to do the show even better than it had been done in the past. The concept of going back to work again on it and making it better seduced me. I went back to work for one season, after which I retired, having accomplished my objective."

Writer David Gerrold, of "The Trouble with Tribbles" fame, and producer Eddie Milkis were also called in. The quartet brainstormed, eventually producing a writer's bible containing input from everyone. Dorothy Fontana was soon brought on board to write the two-hour pilot, and Robert Lewin became writing producer. Artists were hired to provide twenty-fourth-century designs. Andrew Probert set to work on designing the new *Enterprise* (NCC-1701-D); Rick Sternbach updated the STAR TREK props and equipment, while Michael Okuda (whose graphics are now fondly referred to by cast and crew as "Okudagrams") provided a new look for the show's graphics and computers. Bill Theiss, who had created costumes for *The Original Series*, was called in, and George Lucas's Industrial Light and Magic was hired to provide the initial special-effects shots. Academy

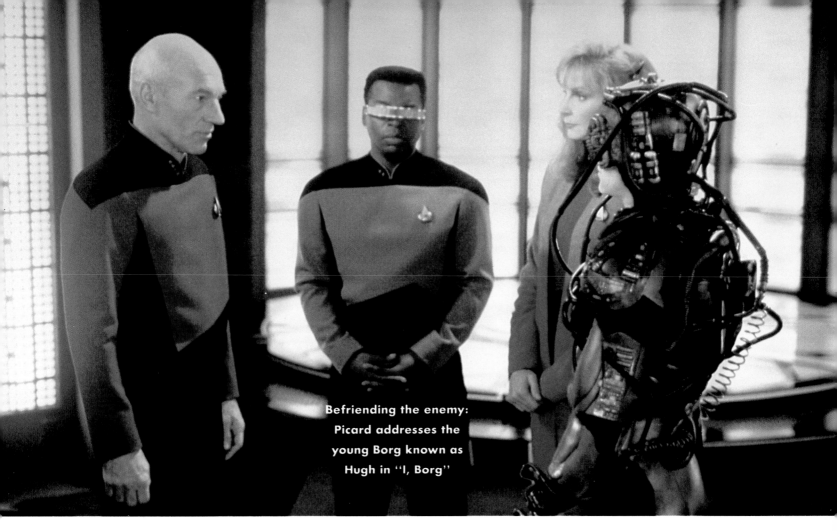

Befriending the enemy:
Picard addresses the
young Borg known as
Hugh in "I, Borg"

Picard consults his old
Academy mentor Boothby
(Ray Walston) in "The First
Duty"

Reinventing the Future

In his book *The World of* Star Trek, David Gerrold listed some of *The Original Series'* logical flaws:

1. The foolhardiness of beaming the captain every week into an unknown, possibly hostile situation.
2. The overly rigid requirement that crew members give up all relationships and family life during the "five year" mission.
3. The much-overused plot device of having the transporter hiccup every other episode.

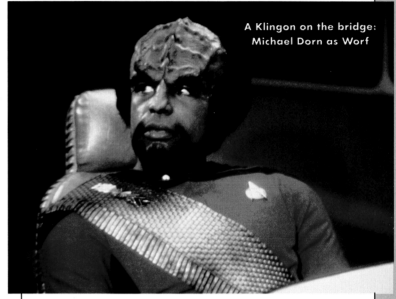

A Klingon on the bridge: Michael Dorn as Worf

When Roddenberry saw that he had a second chance with STAR TREK: THE NEXT GENERATION, he resolved to correct such problems; in addition, he realized that he had to believably update the "Star Trek" universe by almost a century. So he gathered a tried-and-true creative team—*Original Series* producer Bob Justman, *Original Series* head of postproduction Eddie Milkis, and "The Trouble with Tribbles" writer David Gerrold—and began brainstorming. "It was a very homogeneous kind of thing," said Milkis. "We all had input and built off the ideas of each other. Nobody really takes particular credit for anything."

Justman immediately made several suggestions: first, that a Spock-like android and a Klingon warrior should be part of the bridge crew; second, that crew members should be allowed to bring their families along for the duration of the mission. In an early memo, he wrote, "Why should our *Enterprise* crew be denied the opportunity to live a full and rewarding life? Therefore, I propose that we have men, women and children on board through the whole new series. There would be births, deaths, marriages, divorces, etc. . . . What we would have then is, indeed, 'Wagon Train to the Stars.'" Third, Justman suggested that *Enterprise* crew members should have access to a facility that later evolved into the holodeck. He also developed back stories for many of the principal characters.

Of course, not all of his suggestions were immediately embraced. He strongly urged that Wesley Crusher become *Leslie* Crusher, a girl, and also suggested a female science officer, perhaps part Vulcan and a great-great-granddaughter of Spock. Says Justman, "Gene was

very wise. He would listen to people—[some] that he trusted and some that he didn't know—but he would make up his own mind about everything. And if he liked something, then he'd make use of it, and if he didn't he'd throw it away. But Gene had definite ideas; he always had definite ideas!"

Other suggestions that made it: David Gerrold recommended special makeup for the android, perhaps giving him golden skin; he also came up with new methods for calculating warp speed and stardates, and suggested that there be no "dominant" stars, but more of a ensemble feel to the show.

Roddenberry also consulted writer Dorothy Fontana, who urged that the captain's first name be changed from "Julien" to "Jean-Luc," and successfully convinced Roddenberry that the Betazed counselor Deanna Troi should *not* have four breasts. When Fontana heard that Klingons wouldn't be cast as villains, and Roddenberry wanted some new threat to the Federation, "I sent him a memo, suggesting 'How about the Romulans?' After all, they hadn't been developed all that much in *The Original Series*, and they were a glamorous, attractive enemy." Of course, in STAR TREK: THE NEXT GENERATION, the Romulans have since become one of the Federation's strongest adversaries, appearing in more episodes than any other villains.

Dr. Crusher and son: Wil Wheaton and Gates McFadden

Award–winning makeup designer Michael Westmore, who would create Worf's "new" Klingon look as well as that of many other exotic aliens, was brought on board.

Eventually, Roddenberry and company decided on the characters. There was to be the mature, French Captain Picard; his dashing young second-in-command, William Riker; the Pinocchio-like android, Data (then pronounced to rhyme with "that-a"); the tough, Hispanic security chief, Macha Hernandez; the empathic Betazed counselor, Deanna Troi; the blind navigator, Geordi La Forge; the beautiful Dr. Beverly Crusher; and her teenaged son, Wesley.

Obviously, the next order of business was casting. As Robert Justman points out, "In television, casting is everything. Without the proper casting, it doesn't matter how good your premise is. If people won't be drawn to the characters, as portrayed by the actors, then it's all a waste of time.

"It was important that we do the show, that yes it was still STAR TREK, but no these characters are not anything at all like the original characters. And so we set out to create characters that were not replays of the original characters. We didn't build Data to be like Spock. Every character is different. The captain is very different."

Patrick Stewart remembers sensing the producer's indecision about him: "The final reading I did for STAR TREK actually turned into an offer. And it happened so quickly I couldn't be found. After my last reading . . . I went off and had a very, very long breakfast and I read the British newspapers. You know, I

A grinning Riker (Jonathan Frakes) and his Imzadi, Counselor Troi (Marina Sirtis), in "Ménage à Troi"

Casting the Captain, Part II

*T*he first casting decision for STAR TREK: THE NEXT GENERATION was made in an extraordinary way by veteran STAR TREK producer Robert Justman.

One evening, Justman and his wife happened to attend a UCLA lecture series that featured British actor Patrick Stewart. The moment Stewart began to speak, Justman excitedly told his wife, "I think we've just found our captain." As Justman later reported, "once I saw him, that was the captain in my mind. I just couldn't shake it. I've never been so sure of anything as I was with that."

But Roddenberry, who wanted a French actor in the role, failed to share Justman's certainty. In fact, he suggested that the Englishman would be better cast as Data. "I got Patrick Stewart's picture and I looked at it, astonished," Roddenberry recalled. "And I said, 'I'm not going to have a bald Englishman for a captain.' Almost everybody had that reaction. But then I became aware of Stewart's acting ability. And I saw him in a lot of things. The more I saw him, the better I liked him."

Says Justman, "We couldn't find anyone who would satisfy Gene—or ourselves, really—who was good enough. And finally at the end Gene relented and said, 'Well, let's go with Patrick. He's our best choice.'"

The studio shared Roddenberry's hesitancy. Stewart was called back several times, but no commitment was made, so he returned to England. "[Their interest] was not something that I took seriously for one moment," he says. "For every thirty interviews you go for, one of them might turn into an offer. I had no expectations whatsoever." But Stewart was soon summoned back to Hollywood to read for the part again. "And they just said, 'Thank you again,' and I left."

And then Stewart was called back *again*. This time when he arrived in Hollywood, he learned that he was to read wearing a hairpiece. This was Friday evening; Stewart was due to read first thing Monday.

Says he, "I discovered there are things that you can do if you try hard enough. Sunday morning, my wife drove my hairpiece—he's known as 'George,' this hairpiece—to Heathrow, and put it in an envelope into somebody's hand who took it on the plane and took it off. And that afternoon I drove to a little shed somewhere out in the fringes of the Los Angeles airport and picked up George. I remember thinking, 'My God, they better offer me this job after what it's cost me!'"

"The minute we looked at [the toupee], we realized it was wrong," said Gene Roddenberry.

Captain Jean-Luc Picard (Patrick Stewart)

"That wasn't the Patrick we wanted. He looked like a drapery clerk."

So George's cross-Atlantic journey was in vain; fortunately, Stewart's wasn't. He landed the job. "I absolutely didn't expect it at all. Not remotely. I just laughed about the whole thing. Thought it was ridiculous. When I came over to do the pilot show, I didn't unpack my suitcase for a whole month. I had a conviction that one morning they would all simultaneously wake up and say, 'What have we done? We have cast this middle-aged, bald, Shakespearean actor as the captain of the *Enterprise*. We must have been insane!'"

Before the decision to cast Stewart was finalized, another actor by the name of Stephen Macht was being considered for the role of Picard. Dorothy Fontana remembers, "Stephen had played the captain in the film *Galaxina*, a comedy. He's an excellent actor with a craggy face who projects real strength, real masculinity. They called Stephen back [to read for the part of Picard] three times."

Had Macht been cast in the role, says Fontana, "he would have played a very different captain—more American, more direct. And his name probably wouldn't have been Picard!"

Fans who want to see what the *Enterprise*'s captain might have looked like can check out the STAR TREK: DEEP SPACE NINE episodes "The Circle" and "The Siege," in which Macht plays General Krim, a Bajoran military officer.

felt about the audition that, Well, there it is, I've done it. It's now behind me and I've done my best. So I spent a long time . . . over a long leisurely breakfast while my agent and other people were scouring the town looking for me to tell me I got the role. Then, I think, was the most difficult period of thinking hard about the job and thinking about whether it was something I should do."

It wasn't until after he began playing Picard that the full impact of his decision hit home.

"I didn't know . . . that what I was getting involved in was so subtly, deeply, profoundly interwoven into American culture. . . . I didn't know that I was sailing into history with this. . . . For a long time, people would say to me, 'Oh, you're the next William Shatner'—a phrase that used to irritate me at times. Now I see it in its proper perspective. . . . You know, all those original actors have practically become legends."

The next major role cast was that of the *Enterprise*'s first officer, William T. Riker. The producers had difficulty making up their minds in that case, as well.

Jonathan Frakes, who finally landed the role, remembers: "It was a long and winding road. I auditioned seven times over six weeks. I've often said it was harder getting the job than it is doing it. But I was lucky . . . [Roddenberry] took me under his wing after about the fourth audition." Frakes had won supporting roles in the miniseries "North and South," as well as "Falcon Crest" and "Paper Dolls." Prior to STAR TREK, he had just come

Riker in Mintakan garb in "Who Watches the Watchers?"

(*Top row, left to right*) First Officer Riker (Jonathan Frakes), Lieutenant Commander Data (Brent Spiner), Counselor Deanna Troi (Marina Sirtis), Tasha Yar (Denise Crosby); (Bottom row) Geordi La Forge (LeVar Burton), Beverly Crusher (Gates McFadden), Wesley Crusher (Wil Wheaton), and Lieutenant Worf (Michael Dorn)

from doing the stage play *My Life in Art* with Ron Perlman; says he, "We both got something good out of it—I got STAR TREK and he got 'Beauty and the Beast.'"

The next role to be filled was that of Data, an android looking for his creator—a character clearly based on the one in Roddenberry's pilot "The Questor Tapes."

When he was called upon to audition for the part of Data, actor Brent Spiner recalls, "I really didn't know what I was going to do with the character at first because it was just words on a page. They told me that he was an android and that he has superior intelligence and super strength, but it was really a big question mark at that time as to what anybody wanted him to be. It was one of those kind of auditions where you say, 'What is it exactly that you're looking for?' And they say, 'We're looking for an actor who brings something in with him.' . . . To tell you the truth, I didn't even know what an android was!"

Even so, Spiner was hired on the basis of his reading. (Another actor was in serious contention for the role: Eric Menyuk, who so impressed the

Data's evil twin, Lore, outside his compound in "Descent, Part II"

producers that they called him back to guest star as the Traveler in two ST:TNG episodes.) Soon Spiner was being slathered with makeup for screen tests. "I was every color under the sun," he says. "It was unbelievable! I was bubble-gum pink, I was steel gray, I was chartreuse—I was everything! They decided on gold contacts for me finally. I actually see clear through them because the pupils are clear. I also had every kind of wig you could possibly imagine before we settled on my own hair."

Spiner had appeared in several Broadway musicals and in the Woody Allen film *Stardust Memories*; perhaps the role of his best known to television viewers is that of a down-on-his-luck hick on the sitcom "Night Court."

Troi goes undercover as a Romulan in "Face of the Enemy"

Interestingly, British actress Marina Sirtis auditioned not for the part of Counselor Troi, but for Security Chief Hernandez. Bob Justman remembers, "Gene and I saw the movie *Aliens* together. And in [the movie] there was this female with whom Gene was much intrigued. She was a very feisty marine and she played a Latina. She was quite good. [Our character's] name was going to be Macha Hernandez."

But Sirtis brought a warmth and empathy to the reading that the producers decided would work very nicely in the role of Troi. However, had they made the decision to offer her the part one day later, she would have been back in England. As she explains, "The actual day that I was offered the job I was packing to leave. I had been in Los Angeles for six months. I started auditioning for STAR TREK in the middle of March, and at the beginning of May I was due to go back to England because my visa had run out . . . But I had gone out the day before and had bought my family and

A Romulan Warbird

friends gifts and I was ready to go when the phone rang and I was told I got the job. So I unpacked! I was so excited you would have had to scrape me off the ceiling!"

Born in London to Greek parents, Sirtis was interested in acting at an early age; she reports that, at age three, "I used to stand up on the seat of the bus and sing to the other passengers." Her film credits include *The Wicked Lady*, with Faye Dunaway, and *Death Wish III*, with Charles Bronson; she has also appeared on television in "Hunter" and "The Adventures of Sherlock Holmes."

Of course, that left the role of Macha Hernandez to fill; but as Justman notes, "Once we had an 'exotic' for Deanna Troi, it seemed logical to have a different physical type for the head of security."

Enter Denise Crosby, granddaughter of Bing Crosby, whose film credits included *48 Hours* and *Trail of the Pink Panther.* Says Crosby, "I originally

auditioned for the part of Deanna Troi, and
Marina Sirtis auditioned for Tasha Yar [then
Macha Hernandez]. What happened was after
[my] three readings of Troi, Gene Roddenberry
felt that I looked too much like Grace Kelly
and that I looked too much like a wholesome
American girl. He wanted Troi to be a much
more exotic woman but he liked me so much as
an actress, he said, 'Well, what about Tasha?'
And never had the producers considered
someone like me for the role. They envisioned
Tasha as a kind of stocky, tough, dark,
masculine kind of woman. . . . So everyone was

surprised when they casted me for the role." The character was renamed
Tasha Yar, and given a Ukrainian background.

Of all the actors cast on ST:TNG, only LeVar Burton had already
achieved widespread name recognition due to his performance as Kunta
Kinte in the miniseries "Roots." He read for the role of Geordi La Forge
(named by Roddenberry in honor of the late George La Forge, a physically
disabled STAR TREK fan) largely at the suggestion of Robert Justman.
According to Burton, "[Bob Justman] produced a show a long, long time ago
called 'Emergency,' which Gary Lockwood and I starred in. So when STAR
TREK: THE NEXT GENERATION was being cast, Bob brought up my
name and demanded that I be given an audition because he thought I'd be
great on the show."

Of the audition, he says, "I had come to the point in my life where I was ready for anything. So I went there [to the ST:TNG producers' offices] and gave it my best shot. I had a problem at first understanding the role of a blind officer. I tried to act blind while auditioning. The producers took me aside and told me about the VISOR device which allows Geordi to see like anyone else. Then I read the dialogue again with this in mind and apparently they liked the job I did."

Burton also quips, "When the show first started, Geordi was the pilot. It was this great line joke: Here's this blind guy flying the ship . . ."

Actress Gates McFadden, who plays Dr. Beverly Crusher, came with an extensive background in live theater and also as a director-choreographer whose credits include Jim Henson's *Labyrinth* and the fantasy sequences in *Dreamchild*. McFadden reports with a smile that she had a very different idea of Beverly Crusher when she first read for the role. "I thought this was the

Geordi gives his beloved Aquiel (Renée Jones) a piece of his mind

Worf and the Klingon Council
in "Sins of the Father"

A crippled Worf tries to
explain his desire to die to his
son, Alexander, in "Ethics"

funniest female character when I auditioned. I had no idea she was going to be so serious. The scene I auditioned with was the scene from 'Naked Now,' where I was coming on to Captain Picard because of this affliction that made me act drunk, and yet I was trying [unsuccessfully] to be very serious. I thought it was very funny; I thought, This is like Monty Python. Little did I know . . ."

Young actor Wil Wheaton, of *Stand by Me* fame, was cast in the role of her son, Wesley. (It's no coincidence that "Wesley" happens to be Gene Roddenberry's middle name; as he said, "Although I identify with every character, I identify probably more with Wesley Crusher because he is me at seventeen. He is the things I dreamed of being and doing.") Wheaton was absolutely sure he blew his chances of getting the part; as he recalls, "The first time I met Gene was in an audition. I went in the office for the audition and it was my first callback. Well, I sucked! I gave a terrible audition—I

Picard and Beverly share an intimate moment in "Attached"

wasn't focused or anything. I thought to myself, Oh God, I just totally blew this whole wonderful job! I got home and I called my agent and said, 'Please, call them back and tell them I can do a better job. I'll call them and beg if I need to.' Apparently, in the meantime, they had called back and said, 'We know Wil can do a better job. Why don't you bring him back?' I went back on my third audition and I guess I did okay. I auditioned with several of the cast members reading Dr. Crusher's role. I remember that Gene Roddenberry commented about how I wore my shoes untied."

The last part cast was that of Lieutenant Worf—for the very good reason that the character almost didn't make it onto the *Enterprise.*

Worf's loyalties to the Klingon Empire and Starfleet are tested in "Redemption, Part I"

Roddenberry was adamant in not having a retread of *The Original Series*—and that meant no Vulcans, Romulans . . . or Klingons. But Justman persisted, because he felt that having a Klingon on the ship's bridge made an important statement. "Think about what it means to have a *Klingon* officer as part of the crew, as part of Starfleet," he told Roddenberry. "And then it struck Gene; he understood what I was driving at. It shows that, yes, we can make progress."

One of the actors to try out for the part of the Klingon Worf was Michael Dorn, who had been a regular on the series "Chips" and had appeared in the films *Rocky* and *Jagged Edge*. "Joining the cast of STAR TREK: THE NEXT GENERATION was a dream come true," he says. "First, because I'm a Trekkie, and second, I'm playing a Klingon, a character so totally different from the nice-guy roles I've done in the past." Dorn feels that his familiarity with the original STAR TREK series—and thus, Klingons—helped him win the role.

"I was a Klingon when I walked onto the Paramount Studios lot," he recalls. "I didn't joke or talk to the other actors, and I sat by myself. When it was my turn to read, I did not smile, did the reading, thanked them, and walked right out."

With the cast and staff in place, it was time to start production of the pilot. Originally, Dorothy Fontana was to have sole credit on the script for "Encounter at Farpoint," but her script wound up being too short. As she explains, "There was some question as to whether it would be a two-hour show, a ninety-minute show, and even a one-hour show. It was very confusing and hard to plot a story. My basic story wound up being approximately ninety minutes. So Gene said that he would write the prequel, which then became a part of and led into the section that I had written."

Roddenberry added a subplot featuring the enigmatic Q, a character played by John de Lancie, who immediately became popular with the series' fans and returned many times during the show's seven-year run. Fontana also added a touching scene in which Data escorts the 137-year-old Admiral McCoy aboard the *Enterprise*.

DeForest Kelley recollects that "I was at the [Paramount] studio one day and I was walking down the hall and I ran into Dorothy Fontana. So I went into her office to talk with her for a while and she handed me this script and said, 'Would you do me a favor? Would you read this scene?' So I sat down

Suzie Plakson as Worf's first love, Ambassador K'Ehleyr

125

Klingon Spoken Here

When linguist Marc Okrand first agreed to create a few lines of Vulcan dialogue for the movie STAR TREK II: THE WRATH OF KHAN, he had no idea that it would eventually lead to the creation of an entire language for The Original Series' favorite villains, the Klingons—plus *The Klingon Dictionary*, the Klingon Language Institute, and yes, even Klingon Shakespeare.

Okrand had been a fan of *The Original Series*, "though I never followed it on a weekly basis, because I was in college and didn't have a TV." His involvement with STAR TREK initially came about through sheer luck. "I just happened to be visiting Los Angeles having lunch with a friend of mine who was an administrative assistant to Harve Bennett. She and I and another Paramount secretary were having lunch, and in the course of the conversation, it just happened to come out that I had a doctorate in linguistics from Berkeley. And the other secretary said, 'Oh, gee, we've been talking to some people in the linguistics department at UCLA. We're trying to get someone over there to help us with some Vulcan dialogue for a scene in STAR TREK II.' I told her I thought that was great—that they were trying to do it right and not just insert some gobbledygook. 'Yes,' she said, 'but there's a problem in scheduling. We can't seem to get together with this person, and we

have to have this done right away—by the end of this week.' Which just happened to be exactly as long as I was going to be in town. So I said, 'Well, *I* could do that.'"

As fate would have it, at that moment one of the other associate producers for STAR TREK II happened by. The two women told him about Okrand, and he said, "Come talk to us after lunch."

Thus it was that Okrand became STAR TREK's linguist.

The scene to be "translated"—a four-line encounter between Mr. Spock and Saavik—had already been filmed in English. Okrand's task was to match up Vulcan sounds and meanings to the movements of the actors' lips. He did it, and studio executives were pleased with the results.

"So I drove away from it, saying, 'Well, I just taught Mr. Spock to speak Vulcan.' And I thought that was going to be the extent of my involvement [with STAR TREK]."

Far from it. A year and a half later, Bennett called him back to develop a Klingon language for STAR TREK III: THE SEARCH FOR SPOCK. "So the first part of my involvement I owe to luck," says Okrand. "The second part I owe to Harve."

While working on the movie, Okrand decided to go ahead and write what was to become the

The Klingon Council in "Redemption, Part I"

Worf and two renegade Klingons, Korris (Vaughn Armstrong) and Konmel (Charles B. Hyman), perform the Klingon death ritual in "Heart of Glory"

Worf bellies up to a Klingon bar in "Rightful Heir"

Toral (J. D. Cullum), flanked by evil sisters B'Etor (Gwynyth Walsh) and Lursa (Barbara March)

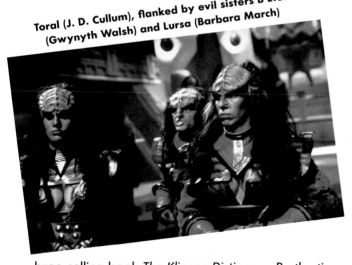

huge-selling book *The Klingon Dictionary*. By the time Okrand was called back to work on STAR TREK V: THE FINAL FRONTIER, STAR TREK: THE NEXT GENERATION was on the air. "The first time they [ST:TNG] ever used Klingon was an episode in the first season, and they made it up themselves. Afterward, they learned about *The Klingon Dictionary*, and they would use it to look for words. When I was doing STAR TREK V, they heard I was on the lot, and consulted me for the episode where

Riker was a 'foreign exchange' student on a Klingon ship."

STAR TREK VI: THE UNDISCOVERED COUNTRY presented an interesting challenge: the translation of Shakespeare into Klingon. "When I showed up on the set, Nick Meyer [the director] said, 'I'm glad you're here. We need 'to be or not to be' in Klingon.' Of course, I had already established and made a big deal out of the fact that the Klingon language possessed no verb that means 'to be.' So I said, 'How about "to live or not to live"?' And Nick said that was okay, so I went to Christopher Plummer. He said, 'I understand you're here to teach me some Shakespeare.'"

The language has proved so popular with fans that a Language Institute was soon formed independently of Okrand (though he's quick to mention that he enthusiastically approves of the organization). Run by Lawrence Schoen, the Institute publishes a quarterly journal, *HolQeD* ("*Linguistics*"), which contains articles in the style of a serious linguistic journal. It also runs a yearly language "summer camp," and members are busily translating the Bible into Klingon. ("They're pretty perturbed with me for not having a word for 'God,'" Okrand jokes.)

But Okrand is quick to point out that Klingon words were first uttered at the very beginning of STAR TREK: THE MOTION PICTURE. "Mark Lenard, who played a Klingon, was the first person to speak Klingon," he says. "And Jimmy Doohan created the lines for him. So the real history of the Klingon language is that it was created by a Federation engineer and first spoken by a Vulcan."

The *Enterprise* crew acts out a
Q-generated Robin Hood
scenario in "QPid"

Q (John DeLancie) takes a
look at what makes Data tick
in "Deja Q"

and read the scene and I said, 'Dorothy, I just don't know whether or not I

can do this. I have a feeling that this show should be *their* show entirely and I

don't know whether an intrusion by me would be appropriate or not.' But I

did tell her that I thought it was a beautiful moment and that I liked it very

much. . . . So then Gene called me and we had lunch together and he expressed his desire for me to do it, too. And I began to think about how much Gene has meant to me . . . I thought it would be . . . a way for me to say thanks for all that he had done for me over the years."

Included in the pilot was Irish actor Colm Meaney, who would go on to become series regular Miles O'Brien on both ST:TNG and *Deep Space Nine*. Meaney read for a part in the new series, but failed to land it; even so, his work won him a background part on the *Enterprise* bridge.

The pilot episode began filming in June 1987. The week of September 28, independent stations began broadcasting the premiere.

Humanity on trial in "Encounter at Farpoint"

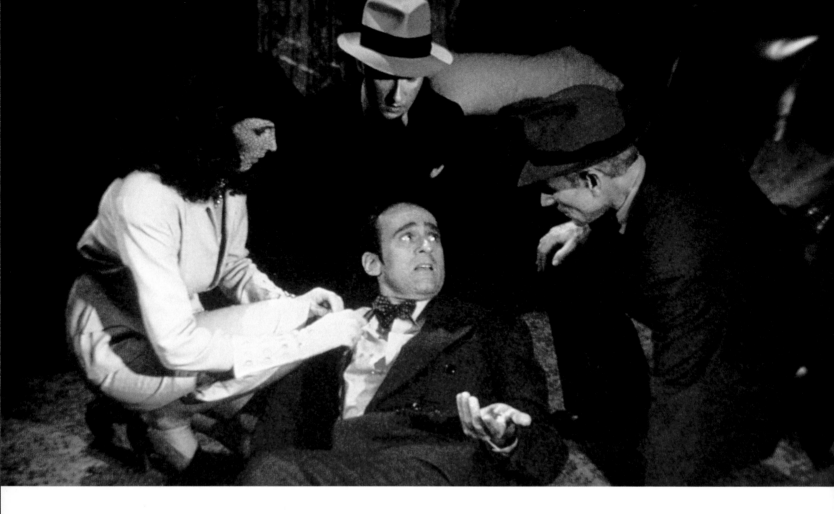

Crusher, Data, and Picard share a Dixon Hill detective romp on the holodeck in "The Big Goodbye"

The majority of reviews were positive; even more so was the viewer response. Ratings showed the ST:TNG pilot beating its prime-time competition in Los Angeles, Dallas, Seattle, Miami, and Denver. Paramount had another STAR TREK success story on its hands.

STAR TREK: THE NEXT GENERATION's first few seasons were marked by change—in both the writing staff and cast. Rick Berman (who came to Paramount in 1984) joined the show as a supervising producer shortly after production began. He recalls, "I had been Paramount's 'studio guy' for the series for about two weeks when Gene Roddenberry asked me to lunch, and it was love at first sight. He went to the studio and said 'Can I have him?' and they said yeah."

But a number of people—especially writers—left. Berman explains, "We were trying hard to put our house in order during the first season. The writers were being rewritten by Gene, and there was a lot of tumult because people didn't know where they stood." In 1987, before production even began, David Gerrold quit the show; Dorothy Fontana soon followed, and not long after, Bob Justman retired. The staff was restructured, with Berman taking on the title of co-executive producer and Maurice Hurley ("Miami Vice," "The Equalizer") becoming the new writing producer; David Livingston took over Justman's job as line producer.

Fresh writing blood was brought in, most notably Tracy Torme (son of singer Mel), whose rewrite of "Haven" brought him a staff job. Torme went on to write one of the most popular first-season episodes, "The Big Goodbye," in which Picard enjoys a 1940s Raymond Chandler–style holodeck romp as detective Dixon Hill. Both Patrick Stewart and Gates McFadden named "The Big Goodbye" as their favorite episode.

There were changes with the cast as well. The episode "Haven" introduced Lwaxana, Troi's outspoken "Auntie Mame" of a mother, played to perfection by Majel Barrett. (Actress Marina Sirtis notes that the character of Troi barely survived during the first season; the writers found the character difficult to write for, and failed to use her at all for four episodes.) By the season's end, actress Denise Crosby, dissatisfied with the role of Yar, departed to pursue a film career. And although press releases stated that Gates McFadden left for similar reasons, in fact, McFadden remembers, "I got a call from my agent saying they had decided to go in another direction with the character. That was literally all I heard. I was very surprised. And my fellow cast members were very surprised."

A libidinous Lwaxana Troi in "Manhunt" (with Carel Struycken as Mr. Homn in background)

Visual Effects in The Next Generation

When a new script is distributed to the STAR TREK production staff, it often calls for visual-effects shots describing fantastic images like "a school of small, flat objects moving in a haphazard manner around each other on a flat plane; the image is beautiful, scintillating, diaphanous—almost not there at all."

Creating such unique images has challenged STAR TREK visual-effects teams since the 1960s, when the Original Series' staff was required to work with traditional optical, or film, effects. "Because of the way effects were done at that time, everything had to be shot optically, even though it was for television," says STAR TREK: DEEP SPACE NINE visual-effects supervisor Gary Hutzel. "Nowadays we [still] shoot everything on film, but we transfer it to D1 videotape and work in the digital realm. It's faster, and we use about one-tenth the number of people to do the same amount of work. That saves a massive amount of money."

Money—or "the Budget," as it is reverently referred to in television and film production—has always been a primary concern in creating a desired shot. According to Gary Hutzel, current STAR TREK effects teams "do the effects for both STAR TREK: THE NEXT GENERATION and DEEP SPACE NINE on shoestring budgets," approximately $85,000 per episode for each series out of a total budget of about $1.2 million per episode, according to studio estimates. Incredibly, this is far less money, when the figures are adjusted for inflation, than the per-episode effects budget of *The Original Series*.

"On *The Original Series* (as well as the first season of *TNG*), they had a lot of problems delivering on film," says Robert Legato, visual-effects supervisor for several seasons of *The Next Generation* and *Deep Space Nine*. In developing *The Next Generation*, Legato notes, "Bob Justman, Peter Lauritson, and Rick Berman said, 'Come up with a faster system.'" That system makes use of videotape to electronically composite the various special-effects elements (a starfield, a planet, and the *Enterprise*, say). This allows the effects to be shot on film and converted to videotape, skipping the costly and time-consuming process called optical printing that puts the elements together.

For the first three seasons of *The Next Generation*, the staff worked in one-inch analog tape format, the prevailing technology at the time. In the fourth season, they switched to the digital format, even though some of the hardware was still considered "research and development," and came without operating manuals. "It's a whole different

Amanda (Olivia D'Abo) contemplates her Q-hood in "True-Q"

An unfortunate Romulan in "Face of the Enemy"

world for visual effects now," Hutzel says. "We regularly do thirty or forty shots per show and have twenty days to deliver it. But when *The Original Series* was being done, literally every effects house in town was booked to do it. Even though many of the episodes had only ten or fifteen of what we would consider 'simple' shots, that was a big deal on that kind of schedule back then."

Today, shots composited in the digital format include motion-control starship shots, transporter beamings, forcefields, viewscreens, computer monitor displays, matte paintings, planets, starfields, nebulas, phaser shots, tractor beams, electricity, creature transformations, and more.

Of course, to save time and money, and to just plain have fun, the staff also makes use of "low

tech" effects, as they did when visual-effects producer Dan Curry created a solar surface by "vibrating dry oatmeal on a light box" and "created the sun's corona by bouncing a laser beam off of a beer can onto a piece of white cardboard."

"I like to do a mixture of low-tech and high-tech," says Curry. "When we have a low-tech option, like a planet texture, I'll do a macro shot of a rock in my garden with my camcorder, and then use it to create the planet surface."

And how would Curry find a low-tech solution for the "school of small, flat objects moving in a haphazard manner around each other on a flat plane" mentioned above? "Shredded-up pieces of white plastic shopping bag, floating in a tub of water!" he quickly responds.

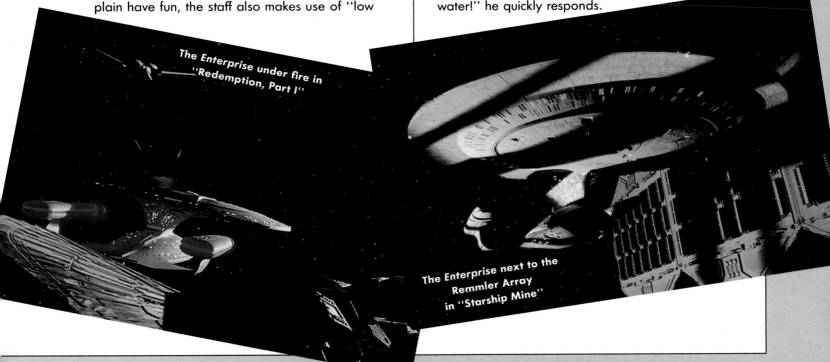

The Enterprise under fire in "Redemption, Part I"

The Enterprise next to the Remmler Array in "Starship Mine"

Dr. Pulaski (Diana Muldaur) enjoys a stroll with "Holmes and Watson" through a holodeck simulation of turn-of-the-century London in "Elementary, My Dear Data"

McFadden was replaced for a season by Diana Muldaur, who played the older, crustier Dr. Kate Pulaski. Muldaur was no stranger to STAR TREK; she had guest-starred in two episodes of *The Original Series* ("Return to Tomorrow" and "Is There in Truth No Beauty?").

But fans missed the Picard/Crusher not-quite-romance, and many wrote Paramount complaining about McFadden's departure from the series. The producers invited McFadden back, and she graciously returned to the series in the third season.

Another second-season addition to the cast was Academy Award winner Whoopi Goldberg. According to Goldberg, "I've always really liked watching STAR TREK. My friend LeVar Burton told me that he was getting ready to do the show and I said, 'Great, let them know I'm interested in doing it.' And, of course, I didn't hear anything for the first year because they thought LeVar was kidding. When I heard that Denise Crosby was leaving, I thought that maybe I could fill that gap—not take her place, but fill a gap—and I hoped that they would let me do it. When they finally realized I was serious, then, of course, everything was expedited—but that's basically how it came to be."

Goldberg describes her character, the mysterious, wise, several-thousand-year-old Guinan, as "a combination of myself, Yoda, and Andrey Sakharov." It was soon established that Guinan knew Q, but "I'm not allowed to say how . . . It would give away why, and what she's doing there on the *Enterprise.*"

Changes in the writing staff continued into the second season. Hannah Louise Shearer, who had come aboard during the first season, left; Leonard Mlodinow and Scott Rubenstein served as story editors until Melinda Snodgrass was hired in that capacity after selling her script "Measure of a Man."

The mysterious Guinan (Whoopi Goldberg)

Picard defends Data's rights in "Measure of a Man"

Sarek and Spock

When Gene Roddenberry was developing STAR TREK: THE NEXT GENERATION, he deliberately set the series nearly one hundred years after the era of the original STAR TREK series, thus guaranteeing it some distance from the characters and situations that gave the first show its identity. Roddenberry clearly wanted his new creation to have its own unique identity. Although some fans were initially disappointed, most gave the show a chance and, just as Roddenberry had planned, came to love the new show for itself.

By the time the series was approaching its third season, it had begun to hit its stride with the public and the fans. Syndicated ratings were climbing, people were excited about the show and its characters, and Roddenberry, reports actor Mark Lenard, felt confident enough to try just what he'd initially set out to avoid.

"I was in Gene's office," recalls Lenard, "and he said, 'You know, it's about time that Sarek comes back. After all, Vulcans age very slowly.'" Lenard notes, "I thought that was a good way to put it, not that they live a long time, but that they age very slowly—because it took them another year and a half before they found a script for me to play!"

That script, titled "Sarek," was tremendously popular with the fans when it aired, and it opened the door to the possibility of the appearance of another "slow aging" Vulcan—in fact, the man who first had put on the pointed ears for the show.

"When we shot 'Unification,'" observes scenic-art supervisor Mike Okuda, "there was a real

Leonard Nimoy returns as Spock

sense for us—and for the audience too, I hope—that Spock's presence on STAR TREK: THE NEXT GENERATION was installing a certain legitimacy on us. It was like *The Next Generation* had come of age. Leonard Nimoy's presence meant a lot to us. I think everyone on the crew shared that feeling."

Mark Lenard again reprised his role as Sarek in that episode, but due to shooting schedules, he did not have the opportunity to work with Leonard Nimoy. He notes, however, that the scenes he performed with Patrick Stewart in both episodes "were a pleasure. Patrick Stewart was very professional—simple, true, clean. There's a great confidence in him that's very important as an actor."

While Lenard enjoyed his small role in "Unification"—"It was a bit like King Lear," he says—he was surprised to discover that the character dies in the two-part episode. "I didn't know," he says. "They only sent me part of the script. So I was at a convention somewhere when the episode aired and I was surprised." While Lenard was touched by the letters he received from concerned fans, he observes that there's no reason why he couldn't appear as Sarek in films set during the original cast's era, or even as another character (he has, after all, also played a Romulan and a Klingon in STAR TREK). And, as Spock once said, there are always possibilities. "Jimmy Doohan, who was at that same convention with me, said to me, 'Well, did anybody see him die? Was anybody there?'" recalls Lenard. "I said, 'No.' 'Well, then,' he told me, 'you're all right!'"

Sarek also joins *The Next Generation*

It was during the second season that the first episode featuring the Borg ("Q Who?" by Maurice Hurley) aired. The Borg, a half-humanoid, half-robot race with a group mind focused on relentless "assimilation" of all other life-forms, proved to be the show's most terrifying—and popular—villains. Over *The Next Generation*'s seven-year course, the Borg would reappear several times in what became landmark episodes.

But it was in the third season that ST:TNG began to come into its own, at least in part due to the arrival of Michael Piller as head of the writing staff. Piller had both written and produced for the TV series "Simon & Simon" (where he coincidentally worked with Maurice Hurley). Says Piller, "I can't claim full credit for [the success]; we had a lot of good writers here. I will claim credit for my contribution, which is that I just have an idea for what I think makes a good dramatic story. . . ."

Picard as the Borg Locutus in "The Best of Both Worlds"

With the combination of Rick Berman and Piller at the helm, magic began to happen. Certainly one who contributed to that magic was STAR TREK fan Ronald D. Moore, whose spec script, "The Bonding," won him the job of story editor. The third season featured some of the show's most popular and powerful episodes, including "Sarek," and Piller's electrifying two-part cliffhanger, "The Best of Both Worlds," in which Jean-Luc Picard undergoes the horrific transformation from human into the cyborg Locutus.

But perhaps the finest and most popular was "Yesterday's *Enterprise*," in which the crippled *Enterprise* 1701-C sails through a temporal rift, thus creating an alternate time line in which Tasha Yar is alive and war exists between the Federation and the Klingons. Eventually, Picard determines that the *Enterprise-C* must return through the rift in order to be destroyed and set history right—and Tasha Yar, who realizes that she should have died in the "correct" time line, volunteers to return with the doomed ship. Perhaps the story's emotional power rests in the fact that Tasha's heretofore senseless death becomes heroic and meaningful.

The story was written by Trent Christopher Ganino and Eric A. Stillwell, who served as script coordinator on the show. The teleplay was

Tasha Yar and Picard consider her fate in "Yesterday's Enterprise"

Future Science

Which came first—the chicken or the egg? Science fiction loves to play with the concept of paradox—the self-contradictory statement that is somehow true, the man who travels into the past to become his own grandfather, the "anomaly" brought into existence by humans that grows larger and larger as it spreads backward through time, until it destroys humanity before *it* has the chance to come into existence (as in the final episode of STAR TREK: THE NEXT GENERATION, "All Good Things . . .").

STAR TREK has become such a significant presence in our cultural gestalt—an anomaly, if you will—that it is occasionally responsible for creating paradoxical situations. *The Original Series,* for example, had such a strong following that in 1976 NASA and the U.S. government was successfully petitioned to name its first experimental space shuttle *Enterprise.* Two years later, film audiences saw a photograph of the real *Enterprise* shuttle on the wall of the fictional *U.S.S. Enterprise*'s recreation deck in STAR TREK: THE MOTION PICTURE, the premise being that the *Starship Enterprise* was the descendant of NASA's space orbiter *Enterprise.* (This amusing conceit continued for several seasons of STAR TREK: THE NEXT GENERATION through the presence of the prop models displayed on the wall of the *Enterprise*-D's conference lounge.) Yet the audience is fully aware that if it hadn't been for the *Starship Enterprise,* NASA's orbiter would not have been named *Enterprise.*

A "chicken and egg" relationship has existed between STAR TREK and the science community for years. "Baby boomers" who were once enraptured by the voyages of Captain Kirk and his crew grew up with the desire to enter the sciences, particularly the space program. Once there, these fans found ways to establish a connection to their original inspiration. For example, longtime STAR TREK fan Mike Coates, captain of the *Discovery* shuttle mission in 1989, persuaded the producers of STAR TREK V: THE FINAL FRONTIER to help him play a little joke on NASA's ground-control team during his flight. Imagine the controllers' surprise when the familiar voice of Captain Kirk was beamed down to them in Houston from the orbiting *Discovery!*

Other members of the scientific community interested in STAR TREK: THE NEXT GENERATION have actually made appearances on that series. Shuttle astronaut Mae Jemison, the first African-American woman in space, portrayed Lieutenant Palmer, a transporter technician, in the sixth-season episode "Second Chances." And one of Data's holographic poker companions in "Descent, Part I" was real-life theoretical physicist Dr. Stephen Hawking.

Hawking's appearance came about after he visited Paramount Studios to help promote the Paramount Home Video release of his *A Brief History of Time.* While on the studio lot, Hawking expressed his desire to see the sets for STAR TREK: THE NEXT GENERATION, a request that was quickly granted by executive producers Rick Berman and Michael Piller, as was Hawking's later wish to sit in the captain's chair on the bridge. Hawking's tour included a stop in Engineering, where he appraised the warp core and noted, "I'm working on that."

Before leaving the studio, Hawking, who does not speak due to the debilitating effect of a neural disease, conveyed to Leonard Nimoy that he would like to be on the show. Nimoy immediately relayed the interest to his friend, Rick Berman. Inspired, Berman and Piller quickly wrote the holodeck scene into "Descent."

The real-life Stephen Hawking, with the holodeck-generated Albert Einstein and Sir Isaac Newton

written by committee—Ira Steven Behr, Richard Manning, Hans Beimler, and Ronald D. Moore—because the final draft had to be written in three short days in order to accommodate a pushed-up shooting schedule. According to Stillwell, "Most of the writers were not very happy with the script. They thought it was going to be horrible, because they don't like having to write [a teleplay] and make it work in three days."

During the fourth season, veteran writer/producer Jeri Taylor ("Quincy," "Magnum P.I.," "Jake and the Fat Man") was hired to do a rewrite on "Suddenly Human." The producers liked her work, and she was offered a position on the writing staff. Soon, she was promoted to producer. Unfamiliar with STAR TREK, she watched ST:TNG and *The Original Series* episodes at a clip of five per night, "until I had pinwheels for eyes."

"I didn't come [to ST:TNG] with an agenda," she says, "but . . . All the stories were about men relating to each other and bonding with each other. I've been able to shore up the roles of Dr. Crusher and Troi, to take them into unexpected directions and out of the traditional roles of caregiver and nurturer . . . [and] I've helped bring, and I say it proudly, romance to the series." Ultimately, after Piller and Berman shifted their emphasis to work on their new series, STAR TREK: DEEP SPACE NINE, Taylor went on to become executive producer.

The stories soon began exploring characters' backgrounds by focusing on family, introducing Worf's brother, son, and adoptive human parents, as well as Picard's brother—and both Tasha Yar's sister and Tasha's half-Romulan daughter, Sela (born as a result of the alternate history begun in "Yesterday's *Enterprise*"). Certainly among the most popular episodes were those featuring the Klingons (beginning with the first season's "Heart of Glory" and continuing with "A Matter of Honor," "The Emissary," "Sins of the Father," "The Reunion," and the two-parters "Redemption" and "Birthright"). Ironically, the Federation's biggest baddies in *The Original Series* were now embraced by STAR TREK fans as the Federation's most adorable group of snarling tough guys.

Soon there was once again a change to *The Next Generation* cast of characters, when Wesley Crusher left for Starfleet Academy at the end of the fourth season. Actor Wil Wheaton explains, "I was offered a few features that were just too good to pass up. I couldn't do them because I was married to the series. I was a little disappointed that they weren't giving me anything

Wil Wheaton as Wesley with Eric Menyuk, who reprised his role as the Traveler in "Journey's End." Menyuk was a top contender for the role of Data

In the episode "Violations," Crusher recalls the day a younger Picard brought her husband's body home

to do." But the door was left open for the character of Wesley to return in guest appearances—which he would (in "The Game," "The First Duty," and "Journey's End").

The series would continue for another four successful seasons before the decision was made to cease producing the series in favor of films featuring the *Next Generation* cast. During those four years, the characters' backgrounds and relationships would continue to be explored, and the series' villains—most notably, the Borg—would be viewed with an unprejudiced eye, one which saw that detente might be possible with even our deadliest enemies. This was the theme of "I, Borg," in which the *Enterprise* crew came to know—and befriend—a young, wounded Borg before making the decision to return him to his people rather than destroy him. Other notable events included the return of James Doohan as Engineer Montgomery Scott in the moving "Relics."

Sadly, creator Gene Roddenberry died during *The Next Generation*'s fifth season, on October 24, 1991, at the age of seventy; but STAR TREK would continue as a lasting tribute to his memory. Fittingly, ST:TNG was enjoying its highest ratings ever, in part due to the airing of "Unification," a two-parter that featured the appearance of Leonard Nimoy as Spock, on a secret mission to the Romulan Empire.

It's interesting to note that two episodes aired not long before Roddenberry's death—"The Wounded" and "Ensign Ro"—would eventually serve as the springboard for yet another new incarnation of STAR TREK.

"The Wounded" delved into the background of Miles O'Brien and the treacherous, predatory Cardassians—and, as ST:TNG was wont to do, humanized the villains by giving us insight into their behavior, while

Gene Roddenberry with two generations of stars in 1991 at the dedication of the new Gene Roddenberry building on the Paramount lot

"Relics" — Rebuilding the Bridge

"**I** really wanted to do the holodeck sequence for 'Relics' on the old bridge," explains Ronald D. Moore, coproducer of STAR TREK: THE NEXT GENERATION and writer of the popular episode. "I sold them on the idea conceptually, but it was a money question. It would be an expensive set to re-create and we weren't going to be able to do it if it cost too much."

Moore asked Michael Okuda, scenic-art supervisor and technical consultant for *The Next Generation*, about the feasibility of re-creating the bridge. A longtime fan of *The Original Series*, Okuda loved the idea, but recognized its difficulty. It was, however, "one of those ideas that ignited everybody's imagination," he recalls.

In researching the project, Okuda's boss, production designer Richard James, soon discovered that there were no accurately scaled drawings of the original set available. Nevertheless, James says, "we started looking at the series and plotting size, trying to get a scope of how big the set was, and how much of it we would need to build." When the initial estimated budget came in too high, James had a brainstorm. "If we could find an episode of *The Original Series* where it has an empty bridge, we could use that as a blue screen process, and then I'd just build a pie-shaped wedge for the live action to be shot against." This, he pointed out to the producers, would be much less expensive, and when Dan Curry, *The Next Generation*'s visual-effects producer, came up with an appropriate shot from the episode "This Side of Paradise," the project was green-lighted by the producers.

Additional cost cutting was achieved when Mike Okuda managed to track down Steve Horch, another avid fan of *The Original Series*. "Steve is a very good model maker, and he had built Chekov and Sulu's console and the captain's chair for use at conventions," says Okuda. "He was kind enough to loan it to us."

James incorporated Horch's pieces into the set, the heart of which was Scotty's engineering station, which also had to serve as the console on the opposite side of the room. "The director, Alex Singer, did a remarkable job of generating different coverage by cheating and using different angles on that one wall," notes Okuda. "Richard James had the clever idea of constructing alternate inserts of the upper panel above Scotty's station, so we could actually change the one screen to two screens when we were pretending it was the opposite direction."

Other contributions were made by set decorator Jim Mees, who found the bases of some classic sixties-style Knoll chairs similar to those that had been used on the bridge, and modified the top portions to match the originals. And professional model maker Greg Jein provided the production with the original buttons that had been used on the consoles. The buttons had been part of a collection of *Original Series* flotsam and jetsam that Jein had picked up from a retired effects man who'd worked on the show.

Incorporating the film footage from "This Side of Paradise" was an equally inspired task. "We got the briefest snippet of this long shot of the bridge from the episode—literally, just a few seconds," says David Takemura, visual-effects coordinator for "Relics." "So

The partial reconstruction of the original bridge

Scotty on the holodeck re-creation of his beloved vessel

we transferred that interpositive to the medium that we work in, digital tape. And we had to cycle that two seconds and print it over and over again to make that background plate long enough for the shot when Scotty walks into the holodeck, which is about a ten-second shot."

"The first shot that we see through the holodeck doors is the scene from 'This Side of Paradise' that is blue-screened in through the holodeck doors," explains Mike Okuda. "The next cut that we see is that same wideshot of the bridge, with Jimmy Doohan blue-screened as if he's walking in the set—an over-the-shoulder shot. Dan Curry and [visual-effects supervisor] David Stipes reviewed the old footage, along with the director of photography Jonathan West. They figured out what kind of lens had been used for the original episode, the camera height, the positions of the lights, so they were able to accurately photograph Jimmy in such a way that he photographically fit into the set."

As difficult as the episode was for all involved, there was a real sense of accomplishment and a sense of carrying on a tradition. "Working on that bridge gave us a real appreciation for the artists that had worked on the original STAR TREK," says Okuda. "We very painstakingly tried to re-create everything, even the 'blinky light' patterns on the consoles, as accurately as possible. And when the special-effects staff fired up the blinkies, the sense of 'this is what it must have felt like to stand on that original bridge' was quite remarkable."

"Relics" — Writing the Story

"**I**'ve always had a love of classic STAR TREK and a love of those characters and of that series," says Ronald D. Moore, coproducer of The Next Generation and writer of "Relics." "It brought me to this show and gave me the job that I have now, so I really wanted to do 'Relics.' It was a privilege to finally give a little something back to something that was very influential in my life."

But how did the idea behind this little gem come about? According to Moore, the saga of "Relics" began when a writer named Michael Rupert submitted a premise to the producers. "He pitched a story where we come across a craft and a man is held in stasis by using the transporter beam," recalls Moore. "We thought that was a neat idea, but we didn't like the story that went along with it. And chatting around the idea of the technical gimmick, [executive producer] Michael Piller came up with the idea of using it as a device to bring back one of The Original Series characters. He suggested Scotty."

After buying the premise from Rupert, Moore was asked to write a story about bringing Scotty to the U.S.S. Enterprise using the transporter gag. "Scotty was a good choice because he's a fun character," says Moore. "He allows you a certain amount of freedom that I think we missed when we had Spock [in the fifth-season two-parter "Unification"]. Spock is a wonderful character, very complex, and yet you could have a little more fun with Scotty . . . he's a joker, he's a little broader, and there was a sense that this could be a lighter episode and be a lot more fun."

Moore's script for the show is full of loving tributes to The Original Series, from Scotty's reminiscences of the Dohlman of Elaas and the "wee bit of trouble" he encountered on his first visit to Argelius (references to

Actor James Doohan with writer Ronald D. Moore

Scotty prepares to raise his glass in a poignant toast to the original Enterprise crew

the episodes "Elaan of Troyius" and "Wolf in the Fold") to Data's comment "It is green," regarding the mystery beverage in Ten-Forward (drawn from Scotty's own comment to an inebriated Kelvan in "By Any Other Name").

But the show's writing had resonance that reached beyond STAR TREK's loyal corps of fans. Episode director Alex Singer recalls that when his wife, "who has no connection to the past of the show," visited the set during the filming of the holodeck sequence, she was moved to tears by Jimmy Doohan's performance as Scotty. And Singer himself had a similar reaction. "I cannot but be moved when Scotty salutes the invisible crew that's not there. I'm not what you'd call a Trekkie, but I sure know what that gesture means. I've lost enough friends and enough of my past that it's a universal gesture. The story was very moving to me."

Ro Laren (Michelle Forbes) looks into the face of her past in "Ensign Ro"

showing that we were just as capable of behaving evilly ourselves. Ensign Ro, a recurring character played by the talented Michelle Forbes, was introduced for reasons explained by Rick Berman: "The other characters in the cast are relatively homogenous; some might even say bland. So we wanted a character with the strength and dignity of a Starfleet officer but with a troubled past, an edge." The "edge" in this case was the fact that the temperamental, headstrong Ro had been court-martialed—and later pardoned—for disobeying orders, an act that led to eight deaths. The Bajoran Ro immediately became popular with the fans, and the story of her people's conflict with the Cardassians would soon form the basis for a new series . . . called STAR TREK: DEEP SPACE NINE.

All Good Things . . .

Only rarely in the history of television does the last episode of a show attract nationwide attention—most shows go out with a whimper, not a bang. Until 1994, only "The Fugitive" and "M*A*S*H" had so touched the hearts of the viewers that their passings were considered a cultural event. Then, in 1994, STAR TREK: THE NEXT GENERATION came to the end of its TV existence, and that ending became an event watched not only by America, but by the world.

Fans everywhere looked on as a chapter in the STAR TREK saga came to a close. The show that had been so much a part of so many people's weekly lives was leaving the air for good. True, it was going on to bigger and better things—STAR TREK: GENERATIONS, the first STAR TREK movie to feature the *Next Generation* cast. Even so, ST: TNG's absence from the small screen was something that was keenly felt, especially by those who worked on the show. "The last day of filming was very emotional for the cast and crew," said Lolita Fatjo, script coordinator for *The Next Generation*. "The behind-the-scenes support staff all stopped what

they were doing and went down to the set to be a part of the final moments of what we all felt to have been one of the greatest times in our lives."

The Next Generation certainly left on a high note, with one of the program's most sweeping and powerful episodes, one that reaches all the way back to the show's beginnings. Seven years ago, Captain Jean-Luc Picard first faced the judgment of the Q Continuum—a race of being with godlike powers over time and space who presumed to gauge humanity's fitness to exist in the galaxy. Seven years ago they suspended judgment, but now their decision has been reached: The human race will be eliminated, not only in the present, but throughout time. Humanity will have never existed.

Picard, of course, finds a way to save the human race, and in the process learns more about himself, the finale being not so much an ending as a beginning. His experience leaves Picard and his crew even better prepared to face their future on the silver screen and whatever challenges may await them out where no one has gone before. . . .

This court is now adjourned: Q as judge in "All Good Things . . ."

Part Five

STAR TREK
DEEP SPACE NINE®

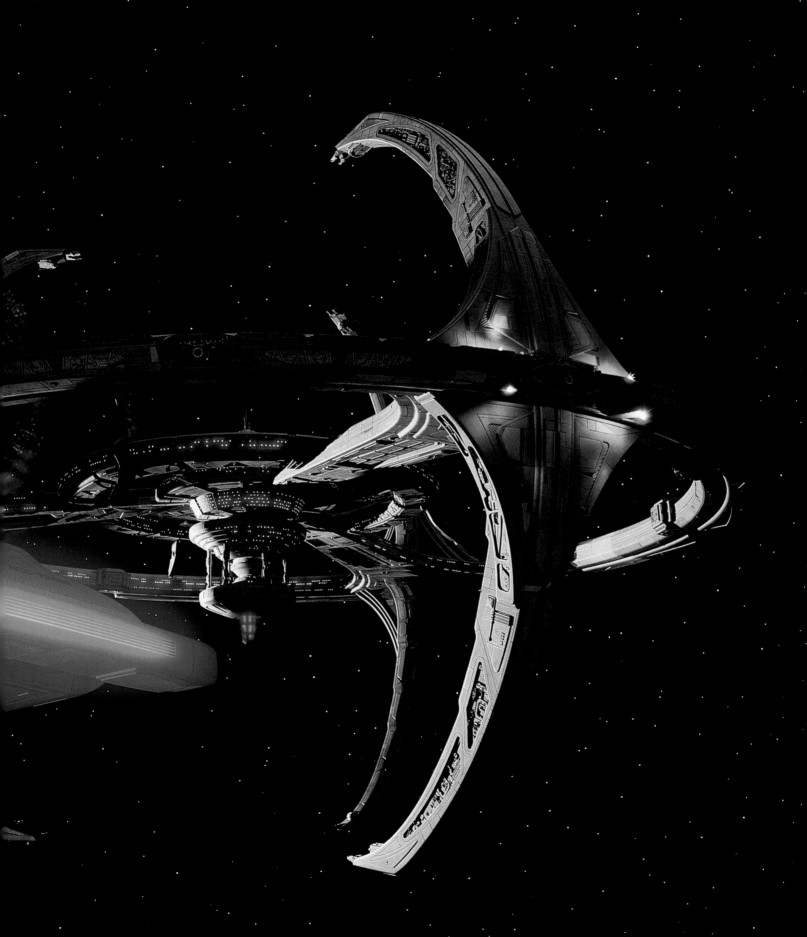

Photography by Gary Hutzel

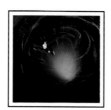

Shortly before Gene Roddenberry's death, in late 1991, Paramount executive Brandon Tartikoff asked Rick Berman to create a new, replacement series for STAR TREK: THE NEXT GENERATION, suggesting that it might be, rather than a "Wagon Train to the Stars," a "Rifleman" in space.

"Do you want to do another science-fiction show or another science-fiction show that is based on STAR TREK?" Berman asked.

"That's up to you," replied Tartikoff.

It just so happened that Berman and Michael Piller had been kicking around ideas for a replacement series—some STAR TREK–based, some not. Berman immediately contacted Piller and the two began brainstorming, ultimately deciding to go with the TREK-based idea.

Says Piller, "If it weren't STAR TREK, we still could have done it, but . . . When it became STAR TREK, it was a real blessing because we could use all of the texture, history, aliens, the entire universe that Gene created. We knew it well and we knew how to make it work, and that allowed us to do several things."

Since the new show would premiere while STAR TREK: THE NEXT GENERATION was still on the air, the pair decided against having a show featuring a crew aboard a starship. And, says Michael Piller, "If you're going to have a show set in space, you basically have three options—on a ship, on an alien planet, or on a space station."

Berman explains, "We had a lot of concerns regarding making a show that was going to be different but not different, making a show that was going to remedy some of the things that were problems on *The Next Generation* but

**Deep Space Nine
in all its glory**

(*left to right*) Station Commander Benjamin Sisko (Avery Brooks), his son, Jake (Cirroc Lofton), and his first officer, Major Kira (Nana Visitor)

doing it without breaking any of Gene's rules. We also had to deal with the problem of doing a STAR TREK show without a starship—trying to do a show based in a stationary location. We had to bring a lot of excitement to that location, and one of the things that Michael and I did was take an entire season of STAR TREK episodes and check to see how many of them could have easily been renovated to work on *Deep Space Nine.* We found that all of them could have been, so there wasn't a big problem there."

The two first considered using a starbase on an alien planet. Almost from the start, they were drawn to the planet Bajor. Part of its appeal had to do with the Bajoran people's conflict with the Cardassians. According to Berman, "We wanted to center the show around Bajor, which was part of the Cardassian Empire. That had been established in 'Ensign Ro,' which was the show that Michael and I had written a year ago. We realized that we certainly couldn't have the Klingons as bad guys and the Borg are not the kind of bad guys that are that practical to use on a regular basis . . . and the Romulans just didn't excite us. So we decided to try to further develop the Cardassians, which will be a continuing process."

They thought of erecting a live-set Bajoran refugee encampment on location, but the cost of leaving the Paramount studio lot would have been enormous. Eventually, they decided on a space station as the most fiscally reasonable solution. But the problem remained as to how to make the location more amenable to an interesting array of guest "aliens" with different conflicts. Hence the concept of a stable wormhole, which would make the space station a hub of activity, frequented by races from all over the galaxy.

The show would be named for the space station—and the title STAR TREK: DEEP SPACE NINE came about, Berman dryly notes, in a very unexciting manner. "We were sitting in my office in one of fifty story

(left to right) Chief of Operations Miles O'Brien (Colm Meaney) and wife, Keiko (Rosalind Chao); and the Trill, Jadzia Dax (symbiont not pictured)

DEEP SPACE NINE as Fort Laramie

On the edge of the frontier, men, women, and children endure a harsh existence. Threatened by the elements, by alien cultures, and sometimes by their own ne'er-do-well comrades, these pioneers struggle to maintain civilization at the edge of their known universe, providing the last touch of home for others who venture out into unknown and unexplored territory.

Welcome to Fort Laramie in the nineteenth century—or to Deep Space Nine in the twenty-fourth.

Just as *The Original Series* was conceived as a "wagon train to the stars," *Deep Space Nine* was conceived as a Western-style outpost in space: located at the edge of the Federation, at the opening to the wormhole that is the only shortcut to the Gamma Quadrant, *Deep Space Nine* is a futuristic mirror of Fort Laramie, a nineteenth-century fortress town located at the entrance to a pass to California.

All the familiar elements of a Western town are represented, in updated, science-fiction form, on *Deep Space Nine*. The sheriff is Security Chief Odo, a loner whose origins are unknown. The owner of the station saloon, the Ferengi named Quark, is the alien version of the nefarious con men who rode the range selling phony maps to nonexistent gold mines, and is the owner of the local brothel—even if the brothel's services are provided via hologram technology, its Western origins are clear. Commander Benjamin Sisko, the head of Deep Space Nine, takes the place of the mayor of the town, and the people of the planet Bajor, trying to rebuild after a devastating alien occupation, are the townspeople he must protect. The presence of the commander's son, Jake, shows that life goes on even

One of the Bad Guys:
The Cardassian Gul Dukat

under less-than-perfect conditions, in a way reminiscent of Chuck Connors's son on the old Western show "The Rifleman."

The gray, unfinished look of the interior of the station adds to the Western-style atmosphere. This is not a glittering, technologically perfect environment—this is a place where people are building what they can and making things work as well as possible, with concern only for getting the job done, and with no time to worry about frills.

As for Indians—the Cardassians, the warlike alien culture that formerly occupied Bajor, provide a similar threat to those on Deep Space Nine. Of course, the station faces threats from across the galaxy and through the wormhole that those inhabiting Fort Laramie in the 1800s could never have imagined.

Yet while the people of the eighteenth century might not have been able to imagine the dangers of life in the twenty-fourth, those pioneers who stood at the edge of the "civilized" New World would have recognized the lifestyle, spirit, and determination of those who choose to make their lives on Deep Space Nine.

O'Brien fights for his life in "Armageddon Game"

  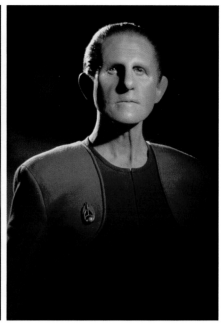

meetings, and we were coming up with various titles and throwing them around. I thought it would be best to name the show after the station that we were designing. Out of my mouth came 'Deep Space Nine.' And Michael Piller looked at me and said, 'Yeah, okay, that will do for now.' We told it to the studio and one person at Paramount liked it and the other thought it wasn't that good. The feeling was 'Well, it will undoubtedly go through the research process and will probably change three times before it gets on the air.' . . . We started calling it *Deep Space Nine* . . . and the promotion people started calling it *Deep Space Nine,* and it stuck!"

It was decided to make *Deep Space Nine* even more different from *The Next Generation* by having the Cardassians (who have grudgingly given up control of Bajor) wreck the space station as they abandon it, as part of their "scorched earth" policy. Credit for that notion goes to Piller, who came up with it as he was writing the first draft of the script. He recalls, "Rick will disagree, but for me the first hour of the pilot [in the first draft] just lay there. It was flat and talky. It was all about introducing the characters and showing

Odo tries to find the truth about Kira's role in a murder in "Necessary Evil"

off Engineering and the Promenade, which looked like the Beverly Center [a glitzy Los Angeles mall]. It had no drama at all. . . . Finally, I went to Rick and said, 'We've got to throw out the first hour.' He said I was crazy. I said, 'There's no drama in a man coming to the space station and deciding to stay.' We had just been struck by the riots and its message was still ringing in our ears. A person who comes to South Central LA, decides to stay, and rounds up the town's people to help rebuild is interesting.

"I said, 'That's drama and that will carry the first hour, but you can't show the beauty of the set and have this concept. You have to blow up the set and then rebuild it during the first show in order for this to work.' That was our one major argument during the script's development." Piller, of course, won.

However, Berman is quick to point out that "in an interview that was given somewhere, some people got the idea that this was going to be a dark and gritty look at the future. I think, in reality, what they were hearing was that it was going to be a dark and gritty space station that our people would take over. The most common question that I have been asked by the press over the last year has been 'Is this show going to be a dark vision of the future?' And I have been constantly telling people that that is incorrect."

The set may be darker and more gothic than that of *The Next Generation*, but the optimistic vision of the future is pure Roddenberry.

Sisko and Jake share a warm, father-son moment in "Playing God"

However, there can be no denying that *Deep Space Nine* has returned to *The Original Series'* "Western" model, with more action and adventure (and a "Dodge City" of a space station). Another difference between *Deep Space Nine* and *The Next Generation:* characters are now allowed to have interpersonal conflicts (something Roddenberry had nixed in *The Next Generation,* insisting that people would be too mature for petty conflict by the twenty-fourth century). According to Brandon Tartikoff's "Rifleman" suggestion, the commander, Benjamin Sisko, would be a single father—faced by the problems not only of unresolved grief and parenting a child alone, but by the massive rebuilding of a devastated planet and space station. And he would often find himself at odds with his second-in-command, a Bajoran national. From the start, Berman and Piller had hoped that that Bajoran would be Ensign Ro, who had appeared in STAR TREK: THE NEXT GENERATION.

Berman recalls, "Before we really started developing the story, we knew that we wanted Michelle Forbes to be part of the show as a Bajoran female. She's an actress we are very fond of and very impressed with. Michelle had just signed a deal to do a feature film and decided she didn't want to commit herself to a series . . . But all this was really before the characters were developed. It's not like we took Major Kira and plugged her into a spot that had been held by Ensign Ro. Basically, once we knew that Michelle wasn't going to be joining us, we sat down and developed our story, and one of the characters that was created was Major Kira."

The creative duo also knew they wanted a character who would serve as a "mirror" of the human condition—an outsider, an alien.

A woman not to be trifled with: Nana Visitor as Kira Nerys

How Far We've Come

From its inception, STAR TREK made a strong commitment to what is now called multiculturalism—a commitment to the idea that by the time humanity spreads outward into space, conflicts based on such trivial things as gender, skin color, and place of origin will be an artifact of the past. It was no accident that STAR TREK presented television's first interracial kiss: it was part and parcel of the basic philosophy of the show.

STAR TREK: DEEP SPACE NINE continues and amplifies this tradition. That the station is commanded by a black man, that his first and second officers are women, that the station doctor is of Middle Eastern descent—these facts are worthy of notice in our society but not in the society inhabited by the characters on the show. To them, this is completely normal: Why shouldn't it be like this? How else would humans behave? This is a smooth continuation of the commitment to forging a better future that has always made STAR TREK unique among American dramatic television series.

Nowhere is this more evident than in the *Deep Space Nine* episode "The Forsaken," when Commander Benjamin Sisko inquires how Dr. Bashir is coping with the assignment he's given him—that of showing a group of obnoxious VIPs around the station. The commander and the doctor have a simple, amusing conversation about the travails of such duties, and how Sisko managed to get his superiors to give that kind of burdensome assignment to someone else. There's nothing unusual about this conversation—it's the kind that goes on every day in offices all over the world. The difference is that when a black man is talking to a Middle Eastern man in a typical television drama, they are almost certain to be talking about drugs, crime, terrorism, or violence—and are most likely to be presented as uneducated, heavily accented, immoral, or antisocial—but never on STAR TREK, where no matter what a character's ethnic background, conversations center around basic human interactions; where educated, articulate professionals of all kinds and colors work together smoothly in pursuit of noble goals; where the color of someone's skin, black or white, blue or orange, says nothing about the content of their character.

It is always far more effective to demonstrate something than to just talk about it, so rather than merely tell us that we *should* all get along, *Deep Space Nine*, following the grand STAR TREK tradition, shows us that we can get along, and that we will—and that we will all be the better for it.

Two Terrans and a shapeshifter

"We wanted someone like that but we didn't want someone to be a carbon copy of Spock or Data," explains Berman. "So we came up with the idea of someone who was not human but who had the guise of a human, the way Data did, but, unlike Data, wasn't all that crazy about being human. We felt that a shapeshifter could provide us with what we wanted—a character who, many years ago, had been forced to take on a human shape out of necessity. . . . We built him a back story and we made him the security chief." Thus the character of Odo was born. And in keeping with the new policy allowing for interpersonal conflict, it only made sense to torment Odo by introducing a Ferengi bartender, Quark, who loved nothing better than to dabble in a few illegal activities while Odo was distracted.

Sisko tries to clear his tight-lipped Trill friend Dax of murder in "Dax"

There were characters that didn't make it: a wheelchair-bound officer from a low-gravity planet who would be enabled to "fly" in a specially created weightless environment (abandoned because the special effects would have proven too expensive on a weekly basis—although she finally appeared in a guest-starring role in "Melora"), and a dual character—a pair of "twins," a male and a female who could only function together. ("I don't know what the hell we were going to do with it," admits Piller, "which is probably why it went away so quickly.")

Other characters that did make it included Jake Sisko, the commander's young son, and the beautiful Jadzia Dax, who belonged to the Trill race already established on ST:TNG. (A Trill is a member of a "joined" species in which the humanoid host body contains a wise, centuries-old "worm," or symbiont.) And as on the previous two incarnations of STAR TREK, there would be a doctor—the brilliant, enthusiastic, and naive Julian Amoros, fresh out of medical school.

And of course, there would be ST:TNG regular (at-the-time) Miles O'Brien.

"We always wanted O'Brien aboard the space station," says Piller. "We loved Colm Meaney as a performer, and we had given him more and more to do on *The Next Generation* over the years. This gives him an opportunity to really explore his character and do some interesting stuff."

Meaney, who has appeared in such films as *The Commitments* and *The Snapper*, was the first principal cast on the new show. He muses that on *The Next Generation* he "had the best of both worlds. There was no commitment either way. I could do *The Next Generation* or I could do films. . . . As a

Going Through Changes

Taya
If I were a changeling, I'd change shape all the time.
Everyone would want to be my friend.
Odo
I wish it were that easy.

— "*Shadowplay*"

*E*veryone marvels at the spectacular images of Odo shifting his shape from his human form to small objects, such as drinking glasses and animals like rats. But what looks like a fast, fluid change in shape is actually the product of a very specialized special-effects team working with state-of-the-art equipment that combines traditional visual effects with the latest computer technology. And each time the special-effects teams who develop his morphing via that equipment get it just right, someone comes up with a new request.

"Unfortunately, Odo is different every time we do a morph," explains STAR TREK: DEEP SPACE NINE visual-effects supervisor Gary Hutzel. "The shots are dreamt up by the writers and discussed during production meetings." The writers decide that Odo will become . . . a chair! a rat! a puddle of bubbling liquid! Something guaranteed to dazzle the television audience. Once the writers agree on the form they want Odo to take, they turn over the shapeshifter's actual manipulation to Hutzel's staff of four.

Hutzel (who handles the effects for odd-numbered episodes) splits the workload on *Deep Space Nine* with fellow visual-effects supervisor Glenn Neufeld (who handles the even-numbered episodes), while both men work under the supervision of visual-effects producer Dan Curry.

For an Odo morph sequence, Hutzel would supervise the shooting on the set, then take the footage to the visual-effects company VisionArt, where he supervises the construction of a three-dimensional computer model of the footage and the final compositing of the various effects elements. "We actually composite it in the 3D environment in the computer."

But what might appear routine at this point seldom is. "It all depends on how Odo's positioned on the 'A' side—where he starts out in the scene—and what he's going to be on the 'B' side,"

says Vision Art production manager Josh Rose. "And, of course, in between he always goes into a transitional state," which the team refers to as a "blobby." "If Odo is morphing into a chair, he first morphs into a 'blobby' shape, which then morphs into the shape of a chair, which then morphs into an actual chair. It's really a series of three or four morphs to turn him into something else."

That basic Odo effect requires use of a 3D image of actor Rene Auberjonois which has been scanned into the computer. The team uses that scan to create a transparent 3D model of Auberjonois's head—or his arm or his entire body, for that matter—onscreen; they then do a 2D "wipe," to paint on surface detail (such as skin). "After the 2D wipe, you see his face," explains Huxtel, "and once we've revealed that, we can do whatever we want to do with it in the computer. We can split it or deform it any way."

"Our 3D software provides a transitional 'blobby' state for Odo to morph to," says Rose. "The morphing software provides morphs between the live action and that blobby state. And often they will shoot Rene against blue screen and then we composit him into the background as well."

This fundamental effect was seen in the pilot episode, "Emissary," when an alien thief throws a knife at Odo. "Rene was shot against blue screen and the knife was shot against blue screen; then we composited those together, with the knife apparently going through him," says Hutzel. "In effect, we had a 3D representation of Rene, which was revealed by the 2D skin wipe, and then we transitioned him into a blobby state and from there we put him wherever he needed to be (away from the knife), and then changed him back into whatever he needed to be (whole again)."

But the shots have grown in their complexity as the series has gone on. In "The Forsaken," Gary

Odo morphs from his familiar form to a spinning top in "Shadowplay"

Hutzel's task was to change Odo into his natural liquid state. "We'd done him as a 3D element," says Hutzel, "But we'd never actually had that turn into just himself." Huxtel had his team "program several thousand 3D spherical shapes and combine their surfaces mathematically, so we had a kind of bubbling, moving essence inside of the glob that poured into Majel Barrett's lap. That effect was something new that we hadn't done before, and it became a new standard."

But on *Deep Space Nine* new standards quickly become old hat. "The original concept behind Odo was that he changed from one thing to another," Huxtel observes. "Now the writers have decided to make him more flexible, so we've had to adjust." For example, in the episode "The Maquis, Part II," the team was asked to help Odo turn his arm into a fluid, stretch it across a room, and yank someone off a ladder. "We'd never done that before," recalls Hutzel. "We had to write special software."

With such care being taken in the effects department, viewers may rest assured that no matter where the writers take the character, Odo's shifts will remain, as Hutzel puts it, "amazing, but not cartoony."

Kira and O'Brien struggle to communicate in "Babel"

freelance actor, you get used to the insecurity of usually not knowing what your next gig will be. After a certain amount of years, that becomes ingrained in you. If someone tries to take that insecurity away from you, you freak a little bit.

"I certainly had that reaction when I was asked to do *Deep Space Nine*. I was doing a lot of features, so I began to think about what I might miss by committing to the show. . . . Two things swung it for me. One, *Deep Space Nine* was a chance to be in town for a long period of time. Two, when you freelance and do a lot of features, you spend seven or eight months on the road going from feature to feature. I have an eight-year-old daughter, and I wasn't seeing much of her or my wife. By doing the show, I could be in town, work, and still get home to them every night.

"Also, the producers have been very cooperative about letting me out to do other things."

But once Colm Meaney was signed, it was time to start casting other actors. The process, Michael Piller notes, "took forever. We thought about people we wanted for Sisko who were just a little too big for us, so we started this huge search."

Says Rick Berman of the casting of Sisko, "Michael Piller and I had discussed at length that we were not going to limit the casting of the lead to a white male. We had decided that we were going to be as open-minded as possible, even to the thought of casting a woman. We thought it would be nice to cast an actor as opposed to a white actor. That left open a lot of people; we saw Asian actors, we saw Latino actors, we saw black actors, white actors, actors from England, Holland, Belgium, Mexico, and a few other countries. We finally got to the point where there were four or five that we thought were the best. We read them for the studio and everyone was in full agreement with Michael and me that Avery Brooks was the best choice for the role. At that point we had to make our only racial decision, which was to hire a black kid to play his son!"

Avery Brooks was no stranger to series television; he had costarred as

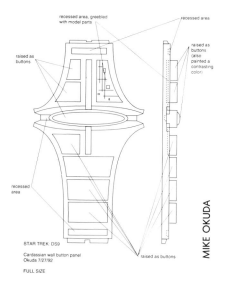

STAR TREK: DS9
Cardassian wall button panel
Okuda 7/27/92
FULL SIZE

MIKE OKUDA

The Cardassian Way:
The Art of Production Design

*H*erman Zimmerman, production designer for STAR TREK: DEEP SPACE NINE, defines a production designer as being ''the person responsible for everything you see on the screen—except for the acting.''

This responsibility requires the intricate meshing of technical knowledge about everything from film stock and camera lenses to visual effects, wardrobe, set, and prop design, all combined with the discerning eye of an artist.

The centerpiece of the series' visual appearance is, of course, the Deep Space Nine space station itself. From the beginning, executive producers and series creators Rick Berman and Michael Piller knew DS9 would have to have the same visual interest and long-term appeal as one of the most durable and beloved settings on television—the *Starship Enterprise*. Gene Roddenberry had always exhorted STAR TREK writers to think of the *Enterprise* as a character, and Berman and Piller set the same conditions for DS9.

Zimmerman's design team had only a few words of description with which to begin their task. In Berman and Piller's treatment for the series' pilot episode, originally titled ''The Ninth Orb,'' the Cardassian space station was simply described as ''a strange, intriguing object in orbit of Bajor.'' The only visual precedent the group had to work from was the look of the Cardassians themselves as they had appeared on *The Next Generation*, with Michael Westmore's exoskeleton makeup, Robert Blackman's carapace-like costumes, and Rick Sternbach's buglike, ''*Galor*-class'' Cardassian warship.

Sternbach credits Rick Berman with giving the design group a key directive for DS9's configuration. ''Berman told us, 'The design has to be as simple and elegant as the *Enterprise*.' '' The executive producer went on to explain that any child can draw the

The distinctive Cardassian silhouette, which first appeared in Michael Westmore's make-up design, has become a hallmark of the Cardassian design aesthetic and the series' overall production design. Note that compared to their orientation in the original design, the wall button panels on the set are used upside down.

Enterprise—a saucer, an engineering hull, two warp engines, and it's done. For DS9, he wanted the same simplicity in the basic shape—something that could be drawn with just a few quick pen strokes.

It took two and a half months for Zimmerman's design team to achieve this goal, and as an example of the all-encompassing vision of production design, the ominous silhouette of the Cardassian exoskeleton is reflected in the station's distinctive docking pylons, the interior Promenade's support pylons, and even in the design of the ubiquitous, wall button panels.

But lines and shapes are not the only consideration a production designer must bear in mind in creating a show's unique visual identity. The storytelling process must also be considered.

Perhaps the most important storytelling feature on the *Enterprise*'s bridge is the visually dramatic main viewscreen. On it, characters can talk to anyone, see near and far, and track their progress through space and the story. Thus, Zimmerman knew a main viewscreen would be an important element of DS9's Ops, just as in the *Enterprise*.

Television's need for rapid story advancement also required a method of getting characters to and from Ops quickly, so the tried-and-true STAR TREK technology of turbolifts was incorporated into the main set's design. Here, though, the turbolifts are not hidden by doors—they can be observed moving up and down with actors on them, reflecting the Cardassian

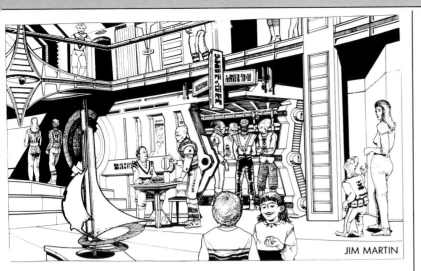

JIM MARTIN

The different design elements of *Deep Space Nine* range from those props which are seen up close and in detail, such as the DS9 station, to background decorations such as this fanciful sign for "Cardassian Sushi," seen hanging on the Promenade.

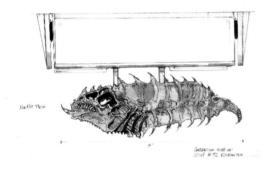

preference for seeing the stark inner workings of their architecture.

How the sets would be filmed also shaped *Deep Space Nine* production-design decisions. Visual-effects supervisor Dan Curry says the technical considerations addressed in the show's planning stages included decisions on lenses, film stock, and exposure, all intended to give the series a slightly different look from that of *The Next Generation*. For example, Curry explains, "*Deep Space Nine* has a darker look. The stars are printed in a little bit darker and the contrast ratio is a little bit greater. If you'll notice, the shadow side of the DS9 station is much darker than the shadow sides of the *Enterprise* under most circumstances. Part of it is that we took our look from NASA orbital shots—real photographs of the space shuttle and other space vehicles. What we ended up with might be termed a grittier look."

Deep Space Nine also boasts intense, saturated colors that arise from the constant use of a slight diffusion filter by director of photography Marvin Rush. As a result, in the midst of high-contrast shadow, the colors on props, costumes, and sets shot on board the station almost appear to glow—another departure from what series co-executive producer Ira Steven Behr calls the "Starfleet-clean" look of *The Next Generation*.

The shape of the space station itself again picks up on Westmore's original makeup design

One of the final design decisions concerned the nature of the graphics to be used on the series. In a move that substantially helped in creating the distinctive visual quality of *Deep Space Nine*, Berman and Piller decided that all equipment on the alien station should be Cardassian, rather than newly installed Starfleet designs. That decision led directly to the use of actual video monitors in the sets, a technique rarely used on *The Next Generation*. With live video there can be constant visual activity in the background of scenes, helping establish Ops, for instance, as a nerve center inundated with information.

Interestingly, the use of contemporary technology such as television monitors in productions set in the future is one of the surest ways to date a science-fiction production. As the series' scenic-art supervisor and technical consultant, Mike Okuda, says, "If the designers of the original STAR TREK series had had the money to use real monitors and the latest in batwing toggle switches, the show would have been obsolete in two years!"

But, within the design team's consistently alien context, which included alien console designs, the twentieth-century television screens became just another element in the overall Cardassian setting—showing how superb production design has created yet another compelling, believable STAR TREK backdrop for the actors who bring *Deep Space Nine*'s stories to life.

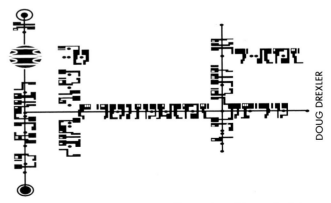

DOUG DREXLER

Though no television viewer will ever be able to decipher Cardassian typography, its distinctive look helps differentiate Cardassian controls from those reflecting Starfleet designs—another example of the detail found in the *Deep Space Nine* environment.

Hawk opposite Robert Urich on "Spencer: For Hire," and played the lead in the spin-off "A Man Called Hawk." Brooks also had a distinguished stage career, performing in *Paul Robeson* and the musical *X: The Life and Times of Malcolm X.* "I grew up watching television," Brooks says. "I don't know that anyone could not be aware of STAR TREK. I certainly was. They sent me the script for *Deep Space Nine,* which I found to be very compelling, so I pursued it. I had to put something on tape for them because I was actually out of the country when they first started to look for an actor to play Sisko. Then

Quark and friends

they asked me to come out to Los Angeles for a test, and I did that. Then they asked me to do the role. Simple enough, thank God."

As Michael Piller notes, "After we cast Sisko, we had pretty good designs on Quark and Odo, and all the other people fell into place."

For Quark, the producers had their eye on Armin Shimerman, who had played a Ferengi on *The Next Generation.* "I like to think I played the first Ferengi [in the ST:TNG episode 'The Last Outpost']," says Shimerman. "There were actually four of us, but in that particular episode, I had the most lines."

Shimerman was an old hand at science-fiction and fantasy series; he played Pascal on "Beauty and the Beast" and had appeared in the television version of *Alien Nation.* (His other television experience includes the role of Cousin Bernie on the short-lived "Brooklyn Bridge.") He credits his getting the roles on both *The Next Generation* and *Deep Space Nine* to casting director Junie Lowry-Johnson, who hired him to play the Ferengi Letek in "The Last Outpost." "Five years later, Junie thought of me for Quark," Shimerman recalls. "She was kind enough to bring me in and push for me to play Quark. I can't thank her enough."

Even though he was thrilled to land the role, Shimerman still felt a great deal of apprehension about having to wear the extensive Ferengi makeup on a daily basis. "So I went to Michael Dorn and I had a chat with him. And Michael gave me some ways to cope with the hours that are spent sitting in the makeup chair. He was very informative—I call him my mentor.

Jake and his best friend Nog concoct a deal

"It's a dream come true to be a part of this," Shimerman enthuses. "It's a dream come true that I can beam up, that I can be part of the legend that I watched as a child, that I revisited when *The Next Generation* came on. Those shows were history long before *Deep Space Nine* was even created. Now I'm a part of all that."

The part of Odo went quickly to veteran actor Rene Auberjonois, probably best known to television viewers as Clayton on the series "Benson." He has also appeared in the films *M*A*S*H*, *The Eyes of Laura Mars*, and *The Ballad of Little Joe*, and had a cameo in STAR TREK VI: THE

Quark and the Ferengi female Bel in "Rules of Acquisition"

UNDISCOVERED COUNTRY as the assassin, Colonel West. "I'm not actually in [STAR TREK VI], technically speaking," Auberjonois admits. "Nicholas Meyer is a friend and he called months before they started it. He said, 'It would be a hoot if you came and did a day's work on it.' . . . I did it as a lark, because Nick is a friend." Auberjonois thought his part had been cut (it had, in the theatrical release) until a STAR TREK convention audience informed him that it had been reinstated in the video version.

He was delighted to get the part of Odo, and says, "My experience with television has always been that the first season takes time to really get going. There is a lot of shakedown, kinks that need to be worked out. With *Deep Space Nine,* I've been astonished at the quality of the scripts from the first

Odo and his mentor, scientist Dr. Mora (James Sloyan), in "The Alternate"

Fast Friends

When Michael Piller began to write the script for the *Deep Space Nine* pilot, "Emissary," he found an interesting interplay between the characters Quark and Odo. It became especially noticeable during the scene when Commander Sisko confronts Quark, who is packing up to leave the space station.

Says Piller, "In that scene Odo is watching Sisko in action and Sisko is doing this number on Quark. Suddenly I found myself writing these asides between Odo and Quark. Quark is saying, 'What do you want me to stay for?' And Odo says, 'I'm a little mystified myself, Commander. The man is a gambler and a thief.' And Quark comes back and says, 'I am not a thief!' And Odo says, 'Yes, you are. You're a thief!'

"Suddenly these guys are going at each other and I realized there's a magic there. These two guys have been archenemies who have been at each other's throats for the last several years—and they love it. They get off on trying to one-up each other and there's a love that comes from within for one another between the good guy and the bad guy that we really explore in the first episode. That's the discovery of character and interaction Rick and I so much wanted to have. It's a conflict that's fun and restores to STAR TREK something that hasn't really been in evidence since the original show."

Many viewers are reminded of the playful sparring between McCoy and Spock, beneath which lurked obvious mutual fondness. But which one—Odo or Quark—plays Spock's "George Burns" to McCoy's "Gracie"?

Clearly, Odo would have to claim the "George Burns" straight-man role. Actor Rene Auberjonois said of his character, "there's a lot of humor in Odo, and the humor comes, not because he's trying to be funny, but because he takes things terribly seriously; especially with Quark, the Ferengi, we're going to see a lot of head butting! Quark and Odo are always getting on each other's nerves. Odo doesn't trust him for one minute! But there is also a sort of grudging respect between the two of them and, in fact, we've already begun to see how, in some ways, they depend on each other."

Armin Shimerman, who plays the greedy Ferengi bartender Quark, called the relationship between Quark and his shapeshifter nemesis, Odo, "wonderful." Before the series premiered, he commented, "I'm hoping the audience will enjoy [the interplay] as much as Rene and I are."

Odo has a friendly little chat with his good pal Quark

episode. The stories are just fabulous. . . . The thing about being a character in a show like STAR TREK, as opposed to, say, 'Benson,' where you know where your character is going to go, is that it's more challenging . . . . With STAR TREK, particularly for me and my character, there's a tremendous amount of variety in the way the character is written, and that really makes my job as an actor much more fun."

Nana Visitor found that getting the part of Kira was no difficulty either; she "nailed the role on the first reading," says Michael Piller, and after the second reading was offered the job.

Visitor was no stranger to series television; she had been a regular on "Ryan's Hope" and "One Life to Live," and had guest-starred on "Murder: She Wrote," "Jake and the Fatman," "Thirtysomething," and "L.A. Law."

The next generation of strong women

A mirror-universe Sisko makes Kira squirm in "Crossover"

She credits Marina Sirtis with helping to set the stage for *Deep Space Nine*'s stronger female characters. "It's very possible that Marina's lobbying and outspokenness about it has benefited the women in *Deep Space Nine*. I was attracted to the script right away by the strength of my character. Actually, both Kira and Dax are powerful women. To play a strong woman on television, or in any medium, really, is unusual, very rare, and it's a huge joy for me."

She had no reservations about committing herself to a possibly long-running series, for as she says, "This is not just an acting job for me. I have a wonderful character to play and I'll be able to play Kira for a long while. I'm not worried about a long run, to tell you the truth. It's a really tough time out there, especially in our business. To be working is great. . . . I'm just thrilled and grateful to be working, and to be working on STAR TREK."

At the suggestion of *Deep Space Nine* films, Visitor exclaims, "Wouldn't that be something? STAR TREK is already a huge part of my life and it always will be. . . . Every role changes you. . . . Every role I've ever done, there has always been a little ghost of it that stayed with me, and I know Kira will, too. I like Kira."

Siddig El Fadil, fairly unknown to American television audiences when he was cast as the young doctor, got the role in an interesting way. Born in the Sudan to British parents of Indian ancestry, El Fadil returned with his family to England shortly after his birth. He soon developed an interest in acting, and got his first break in "Big Battalions," a British miniseries. Soon thereafter, he appeared as King Faisel in "A Dangerous Man, Lawrence After Arabia." Unbeknownst to him, that performance won him the *Deep Space Nine* role. He explains, "['A Dangerous Man'] played here on PBS and I think it was one of the lowest-rated PBS shows ever, but that's the one that Rick Berman saw me in, thank God. Rick's probably one of the few people who saw it. That's what made him think of me for *Deep Space Nine*. So, I can thank that film and its great lighting and direction for me being here now. I'm just glad Rick saw it."

To accommodate El Fadil's background, the young doctor's surname was changed from Amoros to Bashir.

El Fadil recalls with amusement the fact that he once told his agent he wasn't interested in doing series television— unless, of course, he could get a role on STAR TREK: THE NEXT GENERATION. "I was just fresh out of drama school, talking snobbishly and naively, like Bashir. I had only seen one or two episodes of *The Next Generation*. A year later, it was almost to the day, she called me to say, 'Go at ten A.M. tomorrow for your STAR TREK screen test.'"

He's Dead, Ben:
Dr. Bashir in "Vortex"

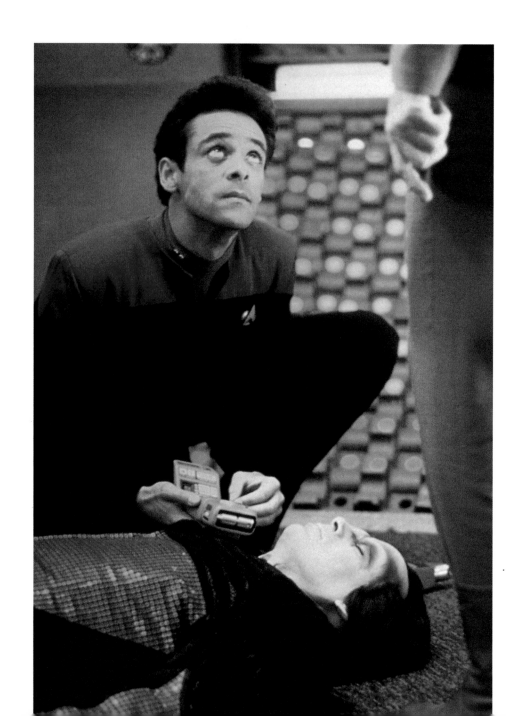

But although the roles of Sisko, Quark, Odo, Kira, and Bashir were filled with relative ease, finding the right actress to play Jadzia Dax proved far more challenging. Michael Piller confesses, "The last one cast was Dax, and it was very difficult to find an actor in that age group with the talent and attractiveness the role required. Terry was . . . one of the last people we saw, and we just fell in love with her and put her on."

Berman agrees: "The most difficult role to cast is always a beautiful girl. It's hard to find one who can act, who doesn't want to bypass television and go into the movies." And part of the problem was conveying the idea of a Trill to those auditioning. "It was difficult to get across that Dax is a beautiful woman and a four-hundred-year-old androgynous creature."

Dax has her symbiont removed in "Invasive Procedures"

Sisko relives an idyllic picnic with his late wife, Jennifer, in "Emissary"

"It was definitely overwhelming in the beginning," says Farrell of her role, "but now I'm getting the hang of it all. . . . As an actress, I just try to look to the oldest, most mature part of myself when I play her [Dax]. They also gave me a tape of 'The Host' [the ST:TNG episode that introduced the Trill race], which I watched several times."

Born in Iowa, Farrell began her career as a fashion model. She appeared on the covers of *Vogue, Mademoiselle,* and many other fashion magazines while she studied acting. She got a costarring role on "Paper Dolls" (on which she worked with Jonathan Frakes). Her other television experience includes guest-starring appearances on "Family Ties," "The Cosby Show," "The Twilight Zone," and "Quantum Leap." Her film credits include *Back to School* and *Hellraiser III.*

"I was so freaked out when I got the part," she admits. "I was so overwhelmed. It was like, 'Oh, my God! This show is the second spin-off of a legend I watched when I was a kid.' It's really a living legend."

Once the cast was finally assembled, the production team went into overdrive during the filming of the pilot, which aired in late January 1993. The two-hour premiere episode of *Deep Space Nine*, "Emissary," received stellar ratings and solid reviews, demonstrating that viewers were hungrier than ever for new STAR TREK stories. And "Emissary" provided all the action and adventure an audience could hope for—plus a character study of Sisko, still tormented by unresolved grief over his wife's violent death.

Lwaxana Troi (Majel Barrett) expresses interest in Odo's unique physiology

Okudagrams

STAR TREK has added dozens of words to our contemporary vocabulary. Items like communicators, phasers, and tribbles are familiar to practically everyone—not surprising in a country where more than fifty percent of the population identify themselves as STAR TREK fans. But behind the scenes of STAR TREK, where even the most serious craftsmen are, alas, only human, these devices were often referred to as "Feinbergers" (after *Original Series* property master Irving Feinberg), "Ruggisms" (for *Original Series* mechanical-effects expert Jimmy Rugg), and, perhaps best known to fans, "the Jefferies tube" (for *Original Series* art director Matt Jefferies).

That tradition is still alive today in the bustling art offices of STAR TREK, where control panels are routinely referred to as "Mees panels," after STAR TREK: THE NEXT GENERATION set decorator Jim Mees, and cryptic notes in scripts refer to most graphics as "Okudagrams," for Michael Okuda, scenic-art supervisor for both *The Next Generation* and STAR TREK: DEEP SPACE NINE.

Okuda began his career with STAR TREK during STAR TREK IV: THE VOYAGE HOME, where he helped to design control panels for the *Starship Enterprise* and the Klingon Bird-of-Prey. Okuda repeated that task for the subsequent STAR TREK films while simultaneously handling his day-to-day chores at *The Next Generation* and, later, *Deep Space Nine*.

Landing the television assignments—he's been involved with both series since their inceptions—was something of a surprise. "Bob Justman, one of *The Next Generation* producers at the time, brought me in for two weeks to do the bridge and the control panels," recalls Okuda. That quickly became six weeks as the producers and production designer Herman Zimmerman worked to establish the look of the new show. Eventually, they realized that graphics were an important part of that look—one that would become an ongoing staple of the show. "They helped convey the futuristic feel and the technological aspects of the scripts," Okuda explains.

The graphics also evolved into an ingenious way to save money in the production budget. "The first few STAR TREK films actually used realistic buttons and control panels, and the cost per square foot was fairly high," says Okuda. "But we developed an approach where we did panels as a backlit graphic transparency and the cost is much, much less. You

EMERGENCY ENVIRONMENTAL SUPPORT MODULE

In case of main and backup power system failure this unit can be activated by opening this panel and pulling the red lever sharply toward you until the first detent.

Pulling the red lever to the second detent will automatically activate all Emergency Support Modules in this immediate section. Maximum operating capacity of this unit is 30 minutes.

EMERGENCY USE ONLY

A panel label Mike Okuda designed for use in STAR TREK VI and STAR TREK: GENERATIONS

also save on the time factor involved. On a feature film, you have many weeks of prep to get ready, whereas in episodic television, you rarely have more than a week. Every advantage suddenly becomes very important."

The average viewer may be aware of Okuda's work only peripherally—the control panel of the transporter, for example, or of the master systems display console in Main Engineering. But the graphics staff is also responsible for readouts, signage, alien written languages, diagrams used in classrooms, the ship's dedication plaque, technical detailing on hand props, and even manipulation of Data's paintings. "Most of the paintings were done by *The Next Generation* scenic-art assistants Jim Magdaleno and Alan Kobayashi or *The Next Generation* art department production assistant Wendy Drapanas," he says, "Again, it's a limitation of time. Wendy once scanned a photo of Data's cat, Spot, into the computer and manipulated the image to make it look like a Picassoesque rendering. That was fun."

The attention to detail that the graphic department's staffs take is also fun, according to Okuda. "We do stationary and animated graphics,

The control panel used to fly the *Enterprise*-D, an example of a backlit display graphic

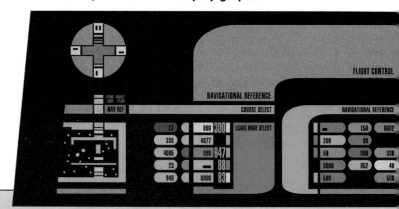

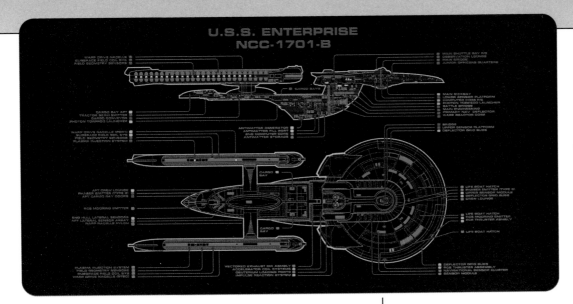

U.S.S. ENTERPRISE
NCC-1701-B

and we try to give all of the readouts the same look, whether it's a static backlit or an animated readout like we use on the *Deep Space Nine* runabouts. You can see the same graphic style, technography, colors, and general layout scheme. I want the viewer to subconsciously be aware that it's all part of the same computer system." On the other hand, although the graphics teams use the same tools to generate graphics for a Federation starship, a Klingon Bird-of-Prey, and a Ferengi Marauder, "we try to give each thing a very different look and feel," to convey the opposite effect to viewers. "That's part of the fun in STAR TREK."

A case in point is the Cardassian space station seen in *Deep Space Nine*. "It was supposed to be a very alien technology and almost incomprehensible to the human eye, so I worked with (*Deep Space Nine* scenic-art assistants) Doug Drexler and Denise Okuda to create this very strange control-panel style, this very strange readout style and colors, like browns and blue-greens, which are very unlike the purples and mauves of Starfleet and the oranges and reds we use for the Klingons."

One symbol from *Deep Space Nine* that astute viewers are seeing a lot of is the oval-shaped Bajoran emblem. "That was actually designed by set designer Nathan Crowley and Doug Drexler. My contribution was that I saw that particular pattern on

one of Nathan's set drawings as a floor plan, and I said, 'That will be our Bajoran symbol.' And then Doug took that basic thing and refined it, and it ended up on the Bajoran communicators." The element has since become a cornerstone of Bajoran design, and is seen incorporated in the architecture of some of the finest Bajoran homes.

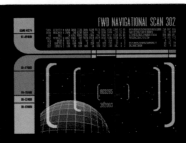

Three examples of Mike Okuda's animated screen displays, seen as computer readouts on TNG and DSN

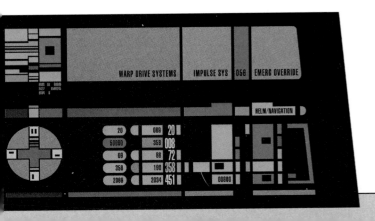

**Kira dons a Vedek's robes in
"The Siege"**

**"The Circle": Kira at Vedek
Bareil's temple**

The combination of character development plus action marked *Deep Space Nine*'s first season. As Rick Berman says, "The first seven shows are very character-based, internal-type shows that explore . . . the community of the space station." Indeed, the very next episode ("A Man Alone") focused on Odo's character. Soon after came an examination of Kira's past and a test of her current loyalties ("Past Prologue"), and the episode "Captive Pursuit," which focused on Miles O'Brien and his friendship with an alien. Also included in that first seven was "Dax," by STAR TREK veteran D. C. Fontana. The first season was also marked by visitors from *The Next Generation:* Q, Vash, and Lwaxana Troi (who lusts after the abashed Odo).

"As the year went on," notes Berman, "we began to feel a little claustrophobic about that [the focus on the space station and its characters] and, for the next group of episodes, we really spread our wings and showed what this franchise was capable of doing. Finally, we ended with some . . . issue-oriented episodes [such as "In the Hands of the Prophets," which took on religious fundamentalism] that showed we could do traditional STAR TREK storytelling."

The following season opened with a bang and a twist—a three-part adventure consisting of the episodes "The Homecoming," "The Circle," and "The Siege," all of which deal with Bajor on the verge of revolution, and Kira's loss of (and return to) her *Deep Space Nine* post. Romance featured prominently in many episodes, with love affairs for Bashir, Quark, and Sisko. The second year also featured the notable return of the original STAR TREK's favorite Klingons—Kor (John Colicos), Kang (Michael Ansara), and Koloth (William Campbell) in the compelling "Blood Oath."

Vedek Winn (Louise Fletcher) and Minister Jaro plot to take control of Bajor and oust the Federation

O'Brien helps rescue Bajorans from a Cardassian prison in ''The Homecoming''

Back in Action

Among the fiercest foes Captain James T. Kirk ever faced were the Klingon officers Kor ("Errand of Mercy"), Kang ("Day of the Dove"), and Koloth ("The Trouble with Tribbles"). Despite the passage of time, these three alien soldiers, played respectively by John Colicos, Michael Ansara, and William Campbell, had never been forgotten by the viewers of STAR TREK. So it was with great excitement that STAR TREK fans everywhere received the news that the three best-known *Original Series* Klingons would be returning to STAR TREK in the STAR TREK: DEEP SPACE NINE episode "Blood Oath."

Now in their declining years, Kor, Kang, and Koloth meet on *Deep Space Nine* to plan one last military campaign, this time of a most personal nature: they have at last located the hidden fortress of the Albino, the renegade Klingon who decades earlier murdered the three warriors' firstborn sons. They have come to *Deep Space Nine* to take on the last member of their party, Jadzia Dax, who, in her previous life as Curzon Dax, had sworn a blood oath to avenge Kang's child, who was Dax's godson and namesake.

The idea of using the old Klingon characters in this episode came up in a conversation between *Deep Space Nine* producer Peter Allan Fields, co-executive producer Ira Steven Behr, and executive producer Michael Piller. "We were quite pleased that all three of these fine actors were willing to reprise their roles," said Fields, who wrote the script for the episode. The return of Kang, Kor, and Koloth was moving and powerful, as these well-known characters go on what turns out to be their final adventure.

This episode provided *Deep Space Nine* with what up to that point was its strongest connection to its roots, weaving it tightly into the universe created in *The Original Series* that is the fundamental underpinning of all things STAR TREK.

Those working on "Blood Oath" felt this special connection being made. Mike Okuda, scenic art supervisor for *Deep Space Nine* said, "At first, you almost didn't recognize them because they were in heavy Klingon makeup. But as soon as Michael Ansara opened his mouth, there was a powerful sense of déjà vu. Having the three *original* Klingons on the show was magical for everyone."

Kor (John Colicos)

Koloth (William Campbell)

Kang (Michael Ansara)

Three grand old warriors on a final mission of honor

Of course, no mention of *Deep Space Nine*'s second season would be complete without the two-part "The Maquis," which introduced a new group of Federation outlaws. It just so happens that the Maquis figure prominently in a certain new television show called STAR TREK: VOYAGER. . . .

At the time these words are being written, *Deep Space Nine* is ending its second successful year. Will it enjoy the same seemingly immortal popularity as its predecessors?

Hard to predict, but it certainly looks good. And, as Rene Auberjonois says, "I'm in it for the long haul. I would love to see the show go six or seven years. Then maybe movies. Who knows?"

Old friends at odds: Starfleet officer-turned-terrorist Cal Hudson (Bernie Casey) and Ben Sisko in "The Maquis, Part II"

Part Six

STAR TREK®

VOYAGER™

AND THE FUTURE

In mid-1993, with plans for transporting STAR TREK: THE NEXT GENERATION from the small-screen to the feature-film format, Paramount Television executives approached Rick Berman with the suggestion that he develop yet another new series. The success of STAR TREK: DEEP SPACE NINE, reports Berman, "had proven that the audience is willing to embrace two STAR TREK shows simultaneously."

Berman quickly pulled executive producer Michael Piller into the conversation. "We were exhausted after just having created *Deep Space Nine,*" says Piller, "and we started by talking about whether we wanted to do it again or not. For a time we thought we might be 'executive consultants,' but we finally said we couldn't go into anything with half a heart—it just wasn't in our makeup. So we said, 'Let's make a go of it.'"

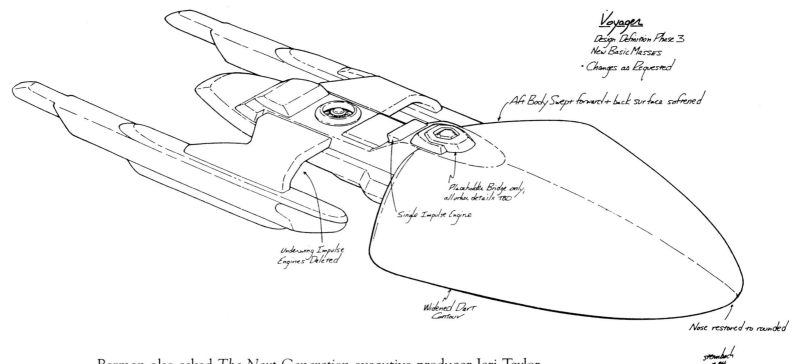

Voyager
Design Definition Phase 3
New Basic Masses
• Changes as Requested

Aft Body Swept forward + back surface softened

Placeholder Bridge only, all other details TBD

Single Impulse Engine

Underwing Impulse Engines Deleted

Widened Dart Contour

Nose restored to rounded

sternbach
4.94

An early design drawing of the *U.S.S. Voyager* by Rick Sternbach

Berman also asked *The Next Generation* executive producer Jeri Taylor to become part of the triumvirate. "I was really gratified," she notes. "Having the ability to create one of the stones in the great wall that is STAR TREK is a great honor in my life."

The trio's discussions resulted in STAR TREK: VOYAGER, "a story that takes place in the same time as *The Next Generation* and *Deep Space Nine*" with "a new class of starship," says Berman. Through a series of circumstances, the *U.S.S. Voyager,* its crew of two hundred, and another ship crewed by a group known as the Maquis are "transported to a portion of space at the edge of the galaxy, a distance that would take seventy or eighty years at warp ten to get home," Berman explains. "Knowing that the galaxy is filled with wormholes and folds in space, our new team of Starfleet officers and the crew of the Maquis ship begin a search together for a way home. They're certainly not going to settle for a seventy-year voyage!"

With their story and setting established, the executive producers "asked ourselves who our captain was going to be, and we decided it might be interesting to make him a science officer," says Piller. "Then we asked ourselves what aliens we'd like to have and we said it might be time to bring a Vulcan back." Recalling that STAR TREK has "always had luck with half-alien/half-human characters," and that "we like writing for Klingons," they also created "a half-Klingon/half-human woman who has trouble controlling the Klingon part of herself." And for the type of character who serves as a mirror of the human condition (such as Spock, Data, and Odo), Piller says, they decided upon an alien couple, "a gentleman's gentleman who is in fact a garbage collector, and his mate, a gorgeous, ethereal creature who has a seven-year life span and an incredible appreciation for each moment of every day."

For extra spice, they briefly considered resurrecting Professor Moriarty, the living holographic character from *The Next Generation* episodes "Elementary, Dear Data" and "Ship in a Bottle," but "everyone agreed that was a little too broad, and we couldn't figure out why anyone would take him along. Then we thought that having a holographic doctor with the full consciousness of being a hologram might be fun, and we'd never done anything like that before, except for Moriarty."

While the executive producers were developing characters, their staff began the task of creating that "new class of Starship." "It's a massive job," says production designer Richard James. "When you look at a blank page, an unlimited number of possibilities come flooding from all directions." But James knew he had to stay within the parameters of established tradition. "STAR TREK has a certain look, and one of our primary goals is to maintain that look as well as to change it. My advice to the people working with me was to consider any idea, no matter how outrageous it might appear to be.

Then we started looking at these ideas and narrowing them down to what fills the bill. The *U.S.S. Voyager* is a newer prototype version of Starship, almost experimental. So it's sleeker-looking, and at the same time it has the lines that would make it look like it evolved from the *Enterprise.*''

Rick Sternbach, senior illustrator on *The Next Generation* and *Deep Space Nine,* designed the exterior of the ship. According to him, "The ship is described in the story bible as a smaller, leaner, meaner starship. My take on it was to borrow shape ideas from things like the *Excelsior* and the runabout from *Deep Space Nine,* but to still keep it STAR TREK. We're not straying too far from the idea of a saucer, a hull, and two nacelles, but it's a more streamlined version."

Grinning, James comments, "I say it's just a little more sexy-looking to me."

On the ship's bridge, James "changed the idea of Conn and Ops and the pilot's position. The pilot will be down front in a pit, eighteen inches lower than the captain's chair and facing about three-quarters to the viewscreen. Con and Ops are on the upper level in opposing niches, and the captain's chair is six inches below that."

Concludes Piller, "It's a tough little mother of a ship. It's built for action and investigation and the hard jobs that the bigger ships are not quite capable of handling. So this ship is commissioned to go in where other ships can't go."

With the basic concepts and characters for *Voyager* in place, the writers began introducing elements of the new series to the STAR TREK audience by seeding the final episodes of *The Next Generation* and late-second-season

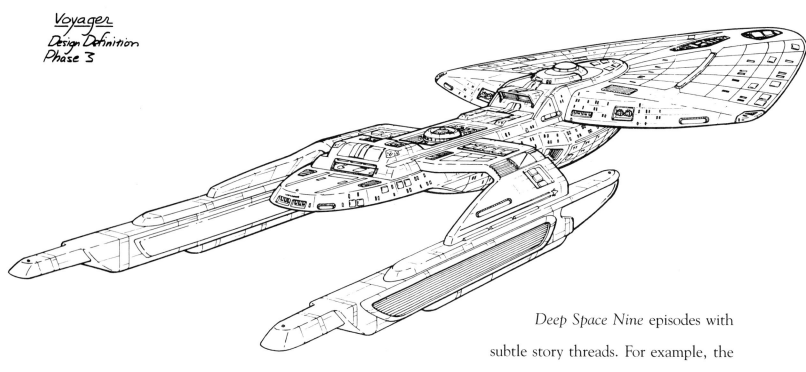

**A more detailed design
drawing of the *U.S.S. Voyager*
by Rick Sternbach**

Deep Space Nine episodes with subtle story threads. For example, the ST:TNG episode "Journey's End" introduced a treaty between the Cardassians and the Federation that established a demilitarized zone and modified territorial borders, thereby requiring some Federation colonists to relocate. The episode focuses on a group of Native American settlers who resist relocation demands—and it's no coincidence that a character who ultimately becomes first officer of the *U.S.S. Voyager* is Native American.

Jeri Taylor explains, " 'Journey's End' was an effort to set up a back story for *Voyager*. We wanted to suggest that there were Native Americans who had moved from Earth to preserve their cultural identity. Our character came from a group like that, but not necessarily the one we saw on *The Next Generation*."

The writers then introduced the Maquis, the group that shares center stage with the crew of the *U.S.S. Voyager*, in a two-part episode on *Deep Space Nine*. "Both parts of 'The Maquis' are back story," Taylor says. The central characters—Federation citizens—refuse to believe that the Cardassians will honor the newly established demilitarized zone, and, but for

Commander Sisko's efforts, almost start a war. "The Maquis may continue to function on *Deep Space Nine,* too," observes Taylor, "but they are a springboard for many of the characters on *Voyager.*"

Michael Piller explains, "We wanted to have some people who are quite different from the Starfleet human types we see all the time, so we created the Maquis, outlaws who are former members of the Federation. They provide a wealth of story material. 'Maquis' was a name used for freedom fighters in World War II, so I thought it might be fun to use it. Essentially we're going to be chasing them when we get caught in this sort of space warp and find ourselves trapped at the edge of the galaxy."

And so, in January 1995, the *U.S.S. Voyager* will go where, once again, no one has gone before. The galaxy provides infinite possibilities for exploration; more than a quarter-century after Gene Roddenberry first conceived of a "Wagon Train to the Stars," STAR TREK's potential for fresh, new stories seems limitless.

With a series of STAR TREK: THE NEXT GENERATION films coming up and the continuing success of *Deep Space Nine,* STAR TREK seems truly immortal. It's easy to envision *Deep Space Nine* going the way of *The Next Generation* and eventually leading to a half-dozen or more theatrical films—followed in several years' time by *Voyager* films, followed by yet another successful STAR TREK series' films . . . One can't help wondering where STAR TREK might be another quarter-century hence.

When asked to speculate, *The Next Generation* executive producer Jeri Taylor replied:

"When Gene Roddenberry first created STAR TREK over twenty-five years ago, he had no way of knowing what a phenomenon it was going to become. He created a series to bring entertainment to people, but it took on a life of its own, becoming greater than the sum of its parts.

"He summed it up when he talked about the crew of the *Enterprise* going boldly forth—and it seems to me that, as we do *Voyager*, we're in somewhat the same position. Part of having an adventure implies that you don't know where you're going. Certainly, Gene didn't know where the *Enterprise* was going in 1966—and we can't say for sure where *Voyager* is going. I think that's part of the wonder and the beauty of STAR TREK, in keeping with the philosophy behind it. If you're going to go boldly into the unknown, then you don't really know where you're going—and if we tried to describe parameters, a goal, or where we might be three years from now, I think we would be shutting out possibilities, and options.

"So part of the risk, and part of the adventure, and part of the excitement, is in not knowing what's coming. You take one step at a time and you take one adventure, and you go from there. That's what we're doing with *Voyager*. We have taken a big risk with cutting ties with everything familiar. The crew of *Voyager* is a long way from home, and they don't know what's going to happen to them; we producers are in the same position. We don't know what's going to happen, and that's the way we like it. . . ."

To quote Captain James T. Kirk of the *U.S.S. Enterprise:* "Risk, gentlemen! That's why we're aboard her . . ."

The future may be unpredictable, but one thing is certain: STAR TREK lives!

Appendix

Star Trek: The Original Series

Production #	Title	Stardate
1	The Cage (1st pilot; never aired)	No Stardate

SEASON ONE

Production #	Title	Stardate
2	Where No Man Has Gone Before (2nd pilot)	1312.4
3	The Corbomite Maneuver	1512.2
4	Mudd's Women	1329.8
5	The Enemy Within	1672.1
6	The Man Trap	1513.1
7	The Naked Time	1704.2
8	Charlie X	1533.6
9	Balance of Terror	1709.1
10	What Are Little Girls Made Of?	2712.4
11	Dagger of the Mind	2715.1
12	Miri	2713.5
13	The Conscience of the King	2817.6
14	The Galileo Seven	2821.5
15	Court Martial	2947.3
16a	The Menagerie, Part 1	3012.4
16b	The Menagerie, Part 2	3012.4
17	Shore Leave	3025.3
18	The Squire of Gothos	2124.5
19	Arena	3045.6
20	The Alternative Factor	3087.6
21	Tomorrow Is Yesterday	3113.2

Production #	Title	Stardate
22	The Return of the Archons	3156.2
23	A Taste of Armageddon	3192.1
24	Space Seed	3141.9
25	This Side of Paradise	3417.3
26	The Devil in the Dark	3196.1
27	Errand of Mercy	3198.4
28	The City on the Edge of Forever	3134.0
29	Operation—Annihilate!	3287.2

SEASON TWO

Production #	Title	Stardate
30	Catspaw	3018.2
31	Metamorphosis	3219.8
32	Friday's Child	3497.2
33	Who Mourns for Adonais?	3468.1
34	Amok Time	3372.7
35	The Doomsday Machine	4202.9
36	Wolf in the Fold	3614.9
37	The Changeling	3541.9
38	The Apple	3715.3
39	Mirror, Mirror	No Stardate
40	The Deadly Years	3478.2
41	I, Mudd	4513.3
42	The Trouble with Tribbles	4523.3
43	Bread and Circuses	4040.7

Appendix

Production #	Title	Stardate
44	Journey to Babel	3842.3
45	A Private Little War	4211.4
46	The Gamesters of Triskelion	3211.7
47	Obsession	3619.2
48	The Immunity Syndrome	4307.1
49	A Piece of the Action	4598.0
50	By Any Other Name	4657.5
51	Return to Tomorrow	4768.3
52	Patterns of Force	2534.0
53	The Ultimate Computer	4729.4
54	The Omega Glory	No Stardate
55	Assignment: Earth	No Stardate

SEASON THREE

Production #	Title	Stardate
56	Spectre of the Gun	4385.3
57	Elaan of Troyius	4372.5
58	The Paradise Syndrome	4842.6
59	The Enterprise Incident	5031.3
60	And the Children Shall Lead	5027.3

Production #	Title	Stardate
61	Spock's Brain	5431.4
62	Is There in Truth No Beauty?	5630.7
63	The Empath	5121.5
64	The Tholian Web	5693.2
65	For the World Is Hollow and I Have Touched the Sky	5476.3
66	Day of the Dove	No Stardate
67	Plato's Stepchildren	5784.2
68	Wink of an Eye	5710.5
69	That Which Survives	No Stardate
70	Let That Be Your Last Battlefield	5730.2
71	Whom Gods Destroy	5718.3
72	The Mark Of Gideon	5423.4
73	The Lights of Zetar	5725.3
74	The Cloud Minders	5818.4
75	The Way to Eden	5832.3
76	Requiem for Methuselah	5843.7
77	The Savage Curtain	5906.4
78	All Our Yesterdays	5943.7
79	Turnabout Intruder	5298.5

Star Trek: The Motion Pictures

Film #	Title	Stardate		Production #	Title	Stardate
1	Star Trek: The Motion Picture	7412.6		5	Star Trek V: The Final Frontier	8454.1
2	Star Trek II: The Wrath of Khan	8130.3		6	Star Trek VI: The Undiscovered Country	9521.6
3	Star Trek III: The Search for Spock	8210.3		7	Star Trek: Generations:	
4	Star Trek IV: The Voyage Home	8390.0			Enterprise B Timeline	9715.0
					Enterprise D Timeline	48650.1

Star Trek: The Animated Series

Production #	Title	Stardate		Production #	Title	Stardate
	SEASON ONE			13	Slaver Weapon	4187.3
1	Yesteryear	5373.4		14	Beyond the Farthest Star	5521.3
2	One of Our Planets Is Missing	5371.3		15	The Eye of the Beholder	5501.2
3	The Lorelai Signal	5483.7		16	Jihad	5683.1
4	More Tribbles, More Troubles	5392.4				
5	The Survivor	5143.3			SEASON TWO	
6	The Infinite Vulcan	5554.4		17	The Pirates of Orion	6334.1
7	The Magicks of Megas-tu	1254.4		18	BEM	7403.6
8	Once Upon a Planet	5591.2		19	Practical Joker	3183.3
9	Mudd's Passion	4978.5		20	Albatross	5275.6
10	The Terratin Incident	5577.3		21	How Sharper Than a Serpent's Tooth	6063.4
11	Time Trap	5267.2		22	The Counter-Clock Incident	6770.3
12	The Ambergris Element	5499.9				

Star Trek: The Next Generation

Paramount Pictures designated the first episode of STAR TREK: THE NEXT GENERATION as production number 101 to differentiate *The Next Generation* episodes from the production numbers for episodes of STAR TREK: THE ORIGINAL SERIES.

Production #	Title	Stardate	Production #	Title	Stardate
SEASON ONE			124	We'll Always Have Paris	41679.9
101	Encounter at Farpoint, Part 1	41153.7	125	Conspiracy	41775.5
102	Encounter at Farpoint, Part 2	41153.7	126	The Neutral Zone	41986.0
103	The Naked Now	41209.2			
104	Code of Honor	41235.5			
105	Haven	41294.5	**SEASON TWO**		
106	Where No One Has Gone Before	41263.1	127	The Child	42073.1
107	The Last Outpost	41386.4	128	Where Silence Has Lease	42193.6
108	Lonely Among Us	41249.3	129	Elementary, Dear Data	42286.3
109	Justice	41255.6	130	The Outrageous Okona	42402.7
110	The Battle	41723.9	131	The Schizoid Man	42437.5
111	Hide And Q	41590.5	132	Loud as a Whisper	42477.2
112	Too Short a Season	41309.5	133	Unnatural Selection	42494.8
113	The Big Goodbye	41997.7	134	A Matter of Honor	42506.5
114	Datalore	41242.4	135	The Measure of a Man	42523.7
115	Angel One	41636.9	136	The Dauphin	42568.8
116	11001001	41365.9	137	Contagion	42609.1
117	Home Soil	41463.9	138	The Royale	42625.4
118	When the Bough Breaks	41509.1	139	Time Squared	42679.2
119	Coming of Age	41416.2	140	The Icarus Factor	42686.4
120	Heart of Glory	41503.7	141	Pen Pals	42695.3
121	The Arsenal of Freedom	41798.2	142	Q Who?	42761.3
122	Skin of Evil	41601.3	143	Samaritan Snare	42779.1
123	Symbiosis	No Stardate	144	Up the Long Ladder	42823.2

Production #	Title	Stardate	Production #	Title	Stardate
145	Manhunt	42859.2	169	Hollow Pursuits	43807.4
146	The Emissary	42901.3	170	The Most Toys	43872.2
147	Peak Performance	42923.4	171	Sarek	43917.4
148	Shades of Grey	42976.1	172	Ménage à Troi	43980.7
			173	Transfigurations	43957.2
	SEASON THREE		174	The Best of Both Worlds, Part 1	43989.1
149	The Ensigns of Command	No Stardate			
150	Evolution	43125.8		SEASON FOUR	
151	The Survivors	43152.4	175	The Best of Both Worlds, Part 2	44001.4
152	Who Watches the Watchers?	43173.5	176	Suddenly Human	44143.7
153	The Bonding	43198.7	177	Brothers	44085.7
154	Booby Trap	43205.6	178	Family	44012.3
155	The Enemy	43349.2	179	Remember Me	44161.2
156	The Price	43385.6	180	Legacy	44215.2
157	The Vengeance Factor	43421.9	181	Reunion	44246.3
158	The Defector	43462.5	182	Future Imperfect	44286.5
159	The Hunted	43489.2	183	Final Mission	44307.3
160	The High Ground	43510.7	184	The Loss	44356.9
161	Deja Q	43539.1	185	Data's Day	44390.1
162	A Matter of Perspective	43610.4	186	The Wounded	44429.6
163	Yesterday's *Enterprise*	43625.2	187	Devil's Due	44474.5
164	The Offspring	43657.0	188	Clues	44502.7
165	Sins of the Father	43685.2	189	First Contact	No Stardate
166	Allegiance	43714.1	190	Galaxy's Child	44614.6
167	Captain's Holiday	43745.2	191	Night Terrors	44631.2
168	Tin Man	43779.3	192	Identity Crisis	44664.5

Production #	Title	Stardate
193	The Nth Degree	44704.2
194	QPid	44741.9
195	The Drumhead	44769.2
196	Half a Life	44805.3
197	The Host	44821.3
198	The Mind's Eye	44885.5
199	In Theory	44932.3
200	Redemption, Part 1	44995.3

SEASON FIVE

201	Redemption, Part 2	45020.4
202	Darmok	45047.2
203	Ensign Ro	45076.3
204	Silicon Avatar	45122.3
205	Disaster	45156.1
206	The Game	45208.2
207	Unification, Part 1	45233.1
208	Unification, Part 2	45245.8
209	A Matter of Time	45349.1
210	New Ground	45376.3
211	Hero Worship	45397.3
212	Violations	45429.3
213	The Masterpiece Society	45470.1
214	Conundrum	45494.2
215	Power Play	45571.2
216	Ethics	45587.3

Production #	Title	Stardate
217	The Outcast	45614.6
218	Cause and Effect	45652.1
219	The First Duty	45703.9
220	The Cost of Living	45733.6
221	The Perfect Mate	45761.3
222	Imaginary Friend	45852.1
223	I, Borg	45854.2
224	The Next Phase	45892.4
225	Inner Light	45944.1
226	Time's Arrow, Part 1	45959.1

SEASON SIX

227	Time's Arrow, Part 2	46001.3
228	Realm of Fear	46041.1
229	Man of the People	46071.6
230	Relics	46125.3
231	Schisms	46154.2
232	True-Q	46192.3
233	Rascals	46235.7
234	A Fistful of Datas	46271.5
235	The Quality of Life	46307.2
236	Chain of Command, Part 1	46357.4
237	Chain of Command, Part 2	46360.8
238	Ship in a Bottle	46424.1
239	Aquiel	46461.3
240	Face of the Enemy	46519.1

Production #	Title	Stardate	Production #	Title	Stardate
241	Tapestry	No Stardate	258	Phantasms	47225.7
242	Birthright, Part 1	46578.4	259	Dark Page	47254.1
243	Birthright, Part 2	46759.2	260	Attached	47304.2
244	Starship Mine	46682.4	261	Forces of Nature	47310.2
245	Lessons	46693.1	262	Inheritance	47391.2
246	The Chase	46731.5	263	Parallels	47410.2
247	Frame of Mind	46778.1	264	The Pegasus	47457.1
248	Suspicions	46830.1	265	Homeward	47553.9
249	Rightful Heir	46852.2	266	Sub Rosa	No Stardate
250	Second Chances	46915.2	267	Lower Decks	47566.7
251	Timescape	46944.2	268	Thine Own Self	47611.2
252	Descent, Part 1	46982.1	269	Masks	47615.2
			270	Eye of the Beholder	47622.1
			271	Genesis	47653.2
SEASON SEVEN			272	Journey's End	47751.2
253	Descent, Part 2	47025.4	273	Firstborn	47779.4
254	Interface	47215.5	274	Bloodlines	47829.1
255	Liaisons	No Stardate	275	Emergence	47869.1
256	Gambit, Part 1	47135.2	276	Preemptive Strike	47941.7
257	Gambit, Part 2	47160.1	277	All Good Things . . .	47988.0

Star Trek: Deep Space Nine

Paramount Pictures designated the first episode of STAR TREK: DEEP SPACE NINE
as production number 401 to differentiate the *Deep Space Nine* episodes
from the production numbers for episodes of the two previous
STAR TREK series.

Production #	Title	Stardate	Production #	Title	Stardate
SEASON ONE			423	The Siege	No Stardate
401	Emissary, Part 1	46379.1	424	Invasive Procedures	47182.1
402	Emissary, Part 2	46379.1	425	Cardassians	No Stardate
403	A Man Alone	46421.5	426	Melora	47229.1
404	Past Prologue	No Stardate	427	Rules of Acquisition	No Stardate
405	Babel	46423.7	428	Necessary Evil	47282.5
406	Captive Pursuit	No Stardate	429	Second Sight	47329.4
407	Q-Less	46531.2	430	Sanctuary	No Stardate
408	Dax	46910.1	431	Rivals	No Stardate
409	The Passenger	No Stardate	432	The Alternate	No Stardate
410	Move Along Home	No Stardate	433	Armageddon Game	47529.4
411	The Nagus	No Stardate	434	Whispers	47581.2
412	Vortex	No Stardate	435	Paradise	47573.1
413	Battle Lines	No Stardate	436	Shadowplay	47603.3
414	The Storyteller	46729.1	437	Playing God	No Stardate
415	Progress	46844.3	438	Profit and Loss	No Stardate
416	If Wishes Were Horses	46853.2	439	Blood Oath	No Stardate
417	The Forsaken	46925.1	440	The Maquis, Part 1	No Stardate
418	Dramatis Personae	46922.3	441	The Maquis, Part 2	No Stardate
419	Duet	No Stardate	442	The Wire	No Stardate
420	In the Hands of the Prophets	No Stardate	443	Crossover	47879.2
			444	The Collaborator	No Stardate
SEASON TWO			445	Tribunal	No Stardate
421	Homecoming	No Stardate	446	The Jem'Hadar	No Stardate
422	The Circle	No Stardate			

Tom Zimberoff

PHOTO CREDITS